DA CAPO PRESS SERIES IN
ARCHITECTURE AND DECORATIVE ART
General Editor: ADOLF K. PLACZEK
Avery Librarian, Columbia University

Volume 39

JACOB HURD AND HIS SONS
Silversmiths

JACOB HURD AND HIS SONS
Nathaniel & Benjamin

Silversmiths
1702-1781

By Hollis French

Foreword by Kathryn C. Buhler

DA CAPO PRESS · NEW YORK · 1972

Library of Congress Cataloging in Publication Data

French, Hollis, 1868-1940.
　Jacob Hurd and his sons Nathaniel & Benjamin,
silversmiths, 1702-1781.
　(Da Capo Press series in architecture and decorative
art, v. 39)
　Inculdes bibliographical references.
　1. Hurd, Jacob, 1703-1758. 2. Hurd, Nathaniel,
1730-1777. 3. Hurd, Benjamin, 1739-1781. I. Title.
NK7198.H8F7 1972　　　739.2′3722　　　70-175722
ISBN 0-306-70406-4

This Da Capo Press edition of *Jacob Hurd and His Sons, Silversmiths* is an una-
bridged republication of the first edition published in 1939 in an edition limited to
250 copies. It is reprinted by special arrangement with the estate of the author.

The *Addenda* printed for the original subscribers in 1941 are reproduced at the
end of this volume.

Published by Da Capo Press, Inc.
A Subsidiary of Plenum Publishing Corporation
227 W. 17th Street, New York, N.Y. 10011

Jacob Hurd

AND HIS SONS

Nathaniel and Benjamin

Silversmiths

1702–1781

NATHANIEL HURD

By Copley

The Cleveland Museum of Art

THE WALPOLE SOCIETY

Jacob Hurd

AND HIS SONS
Nathaniel & Benjamin

Silversmiths

1702 — 1781

By

HOLLIS FRENCH, S.B.

Member of the Walpole Society
Member of the American Antiquarian Society

WITH A FOREWORD BY

KATHRYN C. BUHLER

Assistant in Early American Silver
Museum of Fine Arts
Boston

PRINTED BY THE RIVERSIDE PRESS FOR THE WALPOLE SOCIETY
MCMXXXIX

BY THE SAME AUTHOR

A LIST OF EARLY AMERICAN SILVERSMITHS AND THEIR MARKS
THE THATCHER MAGOUN: AN AMERICAN CLIPPER SHIP

The Riverside Press
CAMBRIDGE · MASSACHUSETTS
PRINTED IN THE U.S.A.

Acknowledgments

THIS WORK is modelled upon the excellent monographs on
'John Coney' and 'Jeremiah Dummer,' written by Hermann
F. Clarke, which are important contributions to our knowledge
of these two provincial silversmiths, their life and works.

If this book should be as successful as Mr. Clarke's, and
would encourage others to write on some of our other early
craftsmen, it would be a source of satisfaction to the author.
There are several silversmiths who would make excellent sub-
jects for additional monographs, and there are certainly a
number of well-informed connoisseurs who have the ability to
write.

While this work has taken from spare time several years of
research, no particular originality is claimed, for it is principally
a compilation of facts that had to be dug from many and varied
records and sources. Persistency was necessary, but without
the help of many experts, it could not have been completed,
and it is a pleasure to record that everyone consulted was most
willing to co-operate.

The author cannot mention all those to whom he is indebted,
as there are too many, but in general he thanks them, as well
as the museums, the libraries, the societies, and the collectors
who have been so generous with their information.

In particular, he must acknowledge the great help given
him by Dr. Harold Bowditch, for information and advice in
connection with the heraldic bookplates of Nathaniel Hurd,
and the coats and crests which appear on so many pieces of
Jacob's and Nathaniel's silver.

There are many of Nathaniel's bookplates and engravings
which could not have been found or indexed without the as-

Acknowledgments

sistance of Mr. Clarence S. Brigham, Secretary of the American Antiquarian Society, who not only placed the treasures of the Society at the author's disposal, but more than that gave generously of his time and knowledge.

He is also under deep obligation to Mrs. Kathryn C. Buhler, of the Boston Museum of Fine Arts, for a great deal of data on Hurd silver and for very helpful advice in the preparation of this book.

To Professor John Marshall Phillips, Curator of the Mabel Brady Garvan Collection, Gallery of Fine Arts, Yale University, he is indebted for most valuable assistance and information, as well as for many photographs of important Hurd pieces and for permission to use them for illustrations.

The library and collections of the Boston Athenaeum have been a mine of information, and the courtesy of their staff, and particularly the research work of Miss Marjorie Crandall, are much appreciated.

The Massachusetts Historical Society through its Librarian, Mr. Allyn B. Forbes, has been very helpful. To Dr. George P. Winship he is indebted for the constructive criticism which has aided in avoiding several pitfalls.

To Miss Winifred M. Beck he is greatly obliged for assistance in the arrangement of the book, and particularly for her research in certain baffling problems, and to Mr. George C. Wales thanks are due for his drawing of the Hurd Blazon reproduced in the text.

HOLLIS FRENCH

ANNISQUAM, 1939

Foreword

By one whose first acquaintance with early American silver, *per se*, was in the excellent company of Mr. French's 'List of Early American Silversmiths and Their Marks' — of which the glossary of terms, not mentioned in the title, was a very thoughtful addition — a further publication by him on a related subject has been eagerly anticipated. In choosing the Hurd family for the subject of his monograph, Mr. French gave himself a difficult task — but one which, by his knowledge and research, he has translated for us into pleasant and fruitful reading.

He begins with the silversmithing *père*, Jacob, the obscurity of whose private life is compensated for and perhaps explained by the abundance of the survivals from his anvil. For busy indeed must have been that Colonial Bostonian who made, to be recorded two centuries later, such a wealth of plate as Mr. French's research has listed to astound us. Jacob's twenty-one teapots presuppose other domestic plate, fashioned for the same families, and in the communion services in New England churches his contemporary reputation as a smith is well exemplified. Meantime, too, he taught two young sons his craft; and did so with such success that one was to surpass his father in the engraving branch of it.

Mr. French's arduously compiled lists of silver give insight into customs of the day: only one teapot by Jacob seems to have an accompanying appurtenance, exclusive perhaps of spoons, i.e., the sugar bowl matching Theophilus Burrill's pot; and from Nathaniel's forge is a teapot and cream jug with matching arms. For sturdier drinking, handles were apparently enjoyed — tankards and cans appear in quantity,

[ix]

Foreword

but only churches had beakers and chalice-type cups from his shop.

Thanks, too, to the rising popularity in the new country of things armorial, Mr. French has given us, in the engravings on silver as well as the splendid section on bookplates, much interesting heraldic data; and, by his own further diligence, interesting biographical sketches of those whose names are still familiar to citizens of Massachusetts as well as many whose present-day obscurity is understandable when one realizes that the world set forth so clearly in Mr. French's book is, after all, almost two centuries removed from this rapid-moving world of today.

KATHRYN C. BUHLER

BOSTON, 1939

Contents

Illustrations

Plates

[xv   ]

Plates

[xvi   ]

Plates

Jacob Hurd

GOLDSMITH

1702–1758

Jacob Hurd, Goldsmith

JOHN HORD, the immigrant ancestor of Jacob, in the fourth generation, must have arrived in Boston not later than 1639, and very possibly earlier. On March 25, 1639, we find an entry in the Boston Town Records which runs, 'John Hord, Taylor, having served Mr Wm Hutchinson, in this town divers years is allowed to be an inhabitant.'

This record is somewhat ambiguous, for it might mean that John had served Hutchinson in England before the latter came to this country, which was in September of the year 1634 on the good ship *Griffin*, or that he had served him 'divers years' afterwards 'in this town.'

It may be argued that, as there is no record of John's obtaining a house lot before 1639, that was the year of his arrival. On the other hand, it was quite customary in those days for a well-to-do gentleman to bring to these shores retainers and tradesmen, paying their passage under an agreement for services to be rendered until the money could be refunded. As there was probably plenty of work for a good English tailor in Boston, at as good or better than London prices from 1634 to 1639, it is quite likely that John came over the seas with William Hutchinson, or shortly thereafter, and by the latter date

[3   ]

had discharged his obligation, and apparently become much interested in land.

Whichever theory is adopted, it is a fact that in 1639 he was recognized as an 'inhabitant.' In the list of members admitted to the First Church, we find the entry, 'John Hurd, a Taylor, and Mary his wife, the 7th of ye 5th Moneth 1639,' so that they became church members, and Savage records that on May 13, 1640, he was admitted freeman and joined the Ancient and Honorable Artillery Company, which gave him his final standing.

It is thought that he came from Shropshire, where there are others of the family who call themselves Hord, Hurd, and Howard, the name meaning a herder, a steward, or a keeper.

We shall speak later of the blazon of the family in England, which is well known, and of the right of the American branch of the family to bear it.

Just where he settled first is a little doubtful, for there are several entries in the old records which are confusing.

In 1639 one entry states that 'on July 29 John Hurd to have a lot for three heads at the Mount.'[1] Another entry states this to be a 'great lott,' and another piece was granted him February 24, 1639/40 and still another January 31, 1641/42.

Whether he actually resided there is doubtful, for he could not well ply his trade unless he were in the town itself. In any event, we find in 1639 that John Leverett granted to John Hurd a 'house lot in exchange for a lot in the henfield,' and that is probably why we find him a little later listed as owning land in Boston.

In 1649 he bought a house and garden and mortgaged it to Governor Dudley for £23, and the same year he bought a small piece of land for 10 shillings at 'ye end of his howse plot.'

Now this property of Hurd's was situated about midway

[1] Meaning for three people at Mount Wollaston.

PLATE I

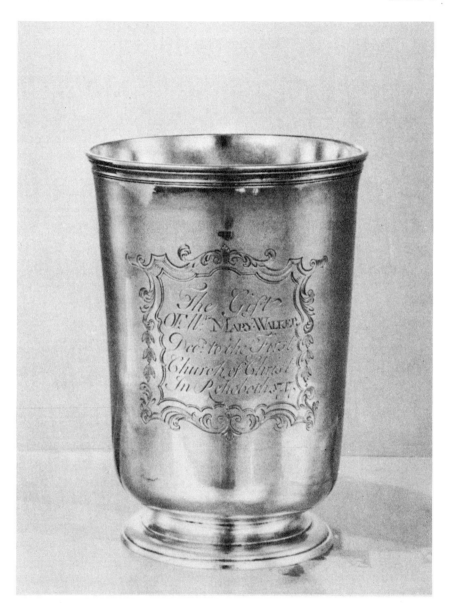

Jacob Hurd, Goldsmith

between Summer and Bedford Streets on Washington Street, probably as part of the land now occupied by Jordan Marsh Company's great store, and here, in a shop built in front of part of his house, John Hurd hung out his tailor's sign and made suits for those other 'inhabitants' and freemen who patronized him.

This location adjoined that of John Hull's father, later occupied by that silversmith himself, who died in 1683, and later again by Samuel Sewall the Diarist, who married Hull's daughter. Hurd was, therefore, in a good location, among pleasant people, and he must have had friendly relations with them, as his will bears evidence.

He was evidently successful, for his will, dated July 11, 1687, describes some property as well as money which he left to his family. His wife was to have the 'sole use profits and improvements' of his estate during her life and after that his oldest son, John Hurd, was to have the 'half of my dwelling house nearest Mr. Hull's land' and 'also the old shop now standing . . . provided y't he forthwith take away and remove it.' 'The other halfe part of my s'd dwelling house . . . with the remainder of my garden and land . . . I bequeath to my son Jacob Hurd.'

He left to his daughter Hannah £5, to his grandson Jacob the same, and 'to all the rest of my Grand Children, twelve pence a peace.'

His will was witnessed, among others, by Jeremiah Dummer, the well-known silversmith and merchant who, with Samuel Sewall, were made 'Overseers' of the will. John signed the will with his mark three years before he died.

Some of his descendants must have resided on John's property up to 1705 when part of it was sold to Bartholomew Green,[1] who printed the *Boston News-Letter*.

The second son, Jacob, who was born in 1653, followed his

[1] Bartholomew Greene, October 12, 1666 — December 28, 1732.

Jacob Hurd, Goldsmith

father's trade, moved to Charlestown, and married Anna Wilson, December 21, 1675, dying on September 7, 1694.

This Jacob was the great-grandfather of Doctor Isaac Hurd, a graduate of Harvard and Harvard Law School, whose name appears in handwriting on one of Nathaniel Hurd's bookplates.

A son of Jacob of Charlestown was a second Jacob, a joiner, who also lived in that town. This grandson of the immigrant John was born September 26, 1676, and died September 23, 1749, having married Elizabeth Tufts. He was appointed 'Ensign in the Second Company of Foot in the Town of Charlestown, whereof Nathaniel Dower is Captain,' by 'Samuel Shute, Captain General and Governour of the Province of Massachusetts Bay.'

He was the father of Jacob, the silversmith, who, though born in Charlestown, lived in Boston until 1755, when we find him in Roxbury. He died in Boston in 1758.

The record, genealogically speaking, of our Jacob, third of the name, is as follows:

JACOB HURD b. February 12, 1703; m. May 20, 1725, to Elizabeth Mason, d. February 17, 1758, N.S. dau. of John and Prudence (Balston) Mason by Rev. Samuel Checkly (Presbyterian) of New South Church. Elizabeth was b. in Boston April 18, 1705, d. June 15, 1764, at 59.

Children:

1. Jacob b. March 1, 1726, Boston; m. Margaret Brown 1760. In 1777 was living in Halifax.

2. John (Col.) b. December 28, 1727; m. 1st, Elizabeth Foster July 24, 1755, d. July 19, 1809. who was b. 1731, d. November 14, 1779.
   2d, Mary Russell Foster, widow of Isaac Foster, on June 8, 1783 (Brattle Church).
   3d, Rebecca Leppington, June 6, 1790 (West Church).

3. Nathaniel b. February 13, 1729, O.S.; d. December 7, 1777. Unmarried.

Jacob Hurd, Goldsmith

4. Elizabeth b. March 17, 1730; m. 1st Daniel Henchman, March 20, 1753
   (New South Church) b. 1731, d. January 7, 1775.
   2d D. Ray or Rae (no issue).

5. Prudence b. and d. August 11, 1732.

6. Prudence b. August 25, 1733; d. April 9, 1736.

7. Ann b. April 5, 1735; m. John Furnass, March 25, 1762.
   d. after 1777.

   Children:

   John Mason Furnass, b. November 11, 1762.
   Nathaniel Hurd Furnass, b. Dec. 10, 1764; m. 1772 Elizabeth, dau.
   of Daniel and Elizabeth Henchman.

8. Prudence b. July 5, 1736; d. January 14, 1737.

9. Sarah b. January 24, 1738; m. December 13, 1767, Thomas Walley as
   second wife. Their son Charles m. Catherine
   Hurd, one of Col. Hurd's twin daughters by
   his second wife, April 3, 1809. Another son,
   Samuel Hall Walley, and daughter, Sally.

10. Benjamin b. May 12, 1739; m. Priscilla Crafts, dau. of Jonathan and
    bap. August 12, 1739.   Susannah (Gore) Crafts, April 13, 1774, who
    d. June 2, 1781.   was b. January 9, 1743, d. November 23,
                              1811.

    Children:

    Benjamin, Jr.
    Sarah, b. November 16, 1779, m. Ebenezer Rhodes; d. June 13, 1870.

11. Mary b. November 4, 1740; d. November 24, 1740.

12. Mary b. November 2, 1742; m. Samuel Hall by Rev. Charles Chauncy,
    June 9, 1766.
    d. Probably before 1777. Not mentioned in Nathaniel's will.

13. Joseph b. February 17, 1744; d. February 1, 1747/8 (Inscription Granary).

14. Prudence b. July 1749; d. September 11, 1749.

The name Prudence, which was that of Mrs. Jacob Hurd's
mother, seems to have been most unfortunate to use for her
grandchildren. One might think that, after naming two children Prudence and losing them, Jacob and his wife would have
tried some other name, but they persisted and even named two
more Prudence and lost them all, for each one of that name
died in infancy.

[7]

Jacob Hurd, Goldsmith

In looking at the records of this period, it is found that they do not always agree as to dates, which is sometimes accounted for by their being written at times in Old Style and again in New Style.

It may be of interest to explain to the reader that, in accordance with the Calendar Act of 1750 of Great Britain, the new calendar went into effect on the 3d of September, 1752, 'Old Style,' which became the 14th by the addition of eleven days, and at the same time the year which had previously begun on March 25, 'Old Style,' thereafter began on January 1 for the 'New Style.' Consequently, for any date between January 1 and March 25, 'Old Style,' we add one year and eleven days, and for any date after March 25, 'Old Style,' we add merely eleven days.

For example, Nathaniel Hurd, who was born February 13, 1729, O.S., requires an addition of one year and eleven days, making his birthday February 24, 1730. He died, therefore, in his forty-eighth year, being actually forty-seven years and ten months old.

Touching Jacob's children, who are listed on page 6, it is interesting that his oldest son Jacob emigrated to Halifax, where he was a 'trader' before 1752, and that his name is still commemorated there in Hurd's Lane.

His daughter Sarah, who married Thomas Walley, became the mother of Sally, who later married John Phillips, the first mayor of Boston, and the two were parents of Wendell Phillips.

There are very limited data on Jacob's life. We do not know to whom he was apprenticed. It might have been Edward Winslow or John Edwards, but in the absence of information it is idle to speculate, though we may say that it was probably neither Dummer nor Coney, for Jacob would have been fifteen years old when the former died and nineteen when Coney died. If he were apprenticed at about fourteen years of age in 1717,

Jacob Hurd, Goldsmith

Dummer would have been seventy-two and Coney sixty-two, both rather old to take apprentices. It may be significant that Jacob was one of the appraisers of John Edwards's estate.

Jacob's name is not found among the students at the Latin School, and we do not know where he was educated.

His public positions were as follows: In 1731 and again in 1736 he was elected Constable, but declined to serve, and paid his fines instead. In 1727 he was chosen Tithingman, and probably served. In 1743, on April 5, he was elected a member of the Ancient and Honorable Artillery Company, then called The Military Company of the Massachusetts, and in 1745 he became First Sergeant, and later he was made Captain in the Boston Regiment, which title he held until death.

In 1733 he lived in Pudding Lane, now Devonshire Street, between State and Water, as is shown by an entry in the Records of the Selectmen (p. 232), as follows:

nov^r. the first 1733

Liberty is Granted To Jacob Hurd of Boston Goldsmith to take up the Pauement and to digg up the Ground in Pudding Lane to Carry His Drain from His House to the comon Shore (sewer) there He making good the Ground and Pauement to the Satisfaction of the Select men and from time to time keeping them in Repair.

It was in 1742 that he lived in a new house on Atkinson Street near Fort Hill, having also at another time dwelt in Cornhill, which is now a part of Washington Street between State and Water Streets, and not the Cornhill we know today, which was laid out in 1816.

In 1735 a petition was circulated requesting subscriptions 'to Erect a Workhouse wherein to employ the Idle and indigent belonging to the Town, which we apprehend a very charitable Undertaking,' etc. Jacob replied to this request by subscribing £5 toward the required £3500.

[9   ]

Jacob Hurd, Goldsmith

Interesting entries in connection with Jacob are found in Samuel Sewall's *Diary*.

Lord's Day, March 28. 1725. In the evening after it, early, My Daughter Cooper was safely deliver'd of a Son, born upon my Birth-Day.

Lord's Day, April 4. Mr. Cooper Baptiseth his Son, and Names him Samuel. It begun now to be his Turn to Baptise. I and my wife, and several more of the family were present. May God bless the child and Teach me to number my Days as to apply my heart unto Wisdom, who am as much above 73. as my little Grandson is old.

June 2. Gave my daughter Cooper for her Son, Samuel, a Silver Spoon weighing one ounce and 12 p.w! Mr. Hurd engraved on the back side of it as in the Margin. S. C. March 28, April, 4. 1725.

From the *News-Letter* and the *Boston Gazette* a few items collected by George F. Dow in his book, *Arts and Crafts in New England*, shed a little light on Jacob Hurd:

JACOB HURD. — Lost, a New Silver Spoon, Mark'd I.L. the maker John (sic) Hurd. Ten Shillings reward and no Questions ask'd. — *Boston Gazette*, Aug. 2/9, 1731.

JACOB HURD, goldsmith, at the south side of the Town house, Boston, advertised a reward of forty shillings for the return of a string of gold beads of small size with a heart stone locket. — *Boston News-Letter*, Sept. 21/28, 1732.

JACOB HURD, silversmith, his large and new house in Atkinson's Street was struck by Lightning, and considerably damag'd, but the Lives of all in the Family were mercifully preserved. — *Boston Gazette*, May 15/22, 1738.

HOUSE STRUCK BY LIGHTNING. — The lightning struck the house of Mr. Jacob Hurd, in Atkinson Street,[1] Boston, and first took off the top of the chimney at the south end of the house, split to pieces the corner balluster, then fell upon the roof and

[1] Now part of Federal Street.

[10   ]

Jacob Hurd, Goldsmith

tore off abundance of shingles, and burst off the plastering into the Garret, then ran down the S.W. corner of the House, tore down the spout and rent off several clapboards, etc. etc. — *Boston News-Letter*, May 18/25, 1738.

JACOB HURD. — Lost or Stolen out of a House in this Town on Tuesday last a Silver Spoon, the Crest of a Pelican upon a Nest feeding her Young, the maker's Name I. Hurd. Whoever brings said Spoon to the Publisher, shall be well rewarded and no Questions ask'd. — *Boston Gazette*, Oct. 16/23, 1738.

JACOB HURD, Capt., goldsmith, formerly of Boston and late of Roxbury, 'being in Town at a Relation's House, was seiz'd with an Apoplexy, in which he continued speechless till Friday Evening, when he departed this Life, Feb. 17, 1758. — *Boston News-Letter*, Feb. 23, 1758 (sup.).

JACOB HURD, Capt. — Boston, Feb. 20. Last Wednesday in the Afternoon Capt. Jacob Hurd, (formerly of this Town,) a noted Goldsmith, was seized with a Lethargy, in which he continued till Friday Evening, and then expired, much lamented. — *Boston Gazette*, Feb. 20, 1758.

Jacob was but fifty-five years old when he died, and considering that he had begotten fourteen children, nine of whom survived, and brought them up in comfort by his trade as silversmith, he must have been a very industrious man.

So far as we know he produced nothing but silver, with the exception of three gold pieces, but it was of a most superior quality. How many pieces he made in all cannot be discovered, but when we remember that a large number must have been worn out, melted, or lost, and when we realize that there must be many in existence today which have not been catalogued, it is plain that his total output, including the 296 pieces indexed herein, must have been greater than that of any other craftsman before or during his time.

It is true that Paul Revere, the patriot, far exceeded this amount, for in the Museum in Boston alone there is a record of nearly that number of pieces, and there are many in other collections besides, but his lifetime was not contemporaneous, as he died sixty years later and lived nearly thirty years longer than Jacob.

Considering the many and valuable pieces which he produced, it is a surprise to find that, in spite of Jacob's great industry, his estate when he died was apparently involved.

While Jacob had a large family to bring up, and hence his expenses must have been heavy, he was evidently able at one time to build for himself a new house in town, and he may possibly have had some losses in real estate transactions, for we find at least a dozen entries in the Grantor Index alone at the Registry.

It would take so much time to puzzle out these transactions that it has not been attempted, but it is noted that, when he bought or built his new house in Cornhill in 1742, he sold his old one 'with land rear Fort Hill on Atkinson St.' the next year for £390 'lawful money of Great Britain.'

It is also evident that he borrowed money from his son John and repaid it before it was due, and that he mortgaged several pieces of property.

However, just what happened is not clear, but Jacob died intestate and his son John was appointed administrator on August 18, 1758, and made two returns to the Probate Court. The first one, dated August 25, 1758, indicated that the assets amounted to only £72–13, while the second one, dated September 1, 1758, just a week later, showed liabilities of £743–6–5½.

Among the debts were items of £447 sterling to William Sitwell and Company (which firm we have not located) and £26–7 to the estate of Edward Winslow, the silversmith, as well as £120 to his son John from whom he evidently had borrowed again.

PLATE II

Jacob Hurd, Goldsmith

In the absence of a final return from the administrator, no definite conclusion can be drawn, but it looks as if Jacob, even with all his industry, had died insolvent.

The mention of these figures brings up the question of the value of colonial money during this period, concerning which the account of Jacob Hurd with Rebecca Townsend is of interest.

The surviving bills of some of the early silversmiths, two of which, one of Jacob's and one of Nathaniel's, are given in the text, are in such apparently large amounts that the question of currency values is naturally raised. The answer to this required a knowledge of the changes in Massachusetts colonial currency, and the question was referred to Miss Ruth Crandall, who has made some study of it in the course of an investigation of prices in Boston during the eighteenth century. Her answer was, in substance, as follows:

> Your surmise (based on the high price of silver quoted in the bills of the Hurds) that there was something radically wrong with the pound is quite correct. That something is what some of our politicians recently tried to foist upon us — paper money inflation. In 1700, ten years after the Massachusetts legislature had started down that rosy path, but before the roses had thrust out their thorns, the price of an ounce of silver was about seven shillings in either paper or hard money. By 1749, just before the return to honest money, that price had risen to 60 shillings in paper, and hard money had disappeared.
>
> Jacob's bill to Mrs. Townsend gives its own evidence that in 1746/47 silver was selling in Boston for 50 shillings an ounce. The form of currency was not mentioned, for at that time all accounts were transacted through the medium of paper money of old tenor and there was no need to mention the fact.
>
> This price of 50 shillings per ounce indicated an inflation of about 700 per cent. Thus the £5 charge against Rebecca for fashioning her 6 tea spoons and tongs was worth one seventh, or only 14.3s in hard money, while her credit of about £23 5/ for

Mrs Rebeccah Townsend to Jacob Hurd

Dr			Cr	
1740				
June 5	To 1 Sett Stone Buttons - - - - - - - - - -	2. .	By Old Buckles - - - - - - - - - - - - - -	£.1.10
1741			1746	
May 4	To 1 pr Buckles - - - - - -	3.10	Aug 15 By Silver 9^{oz} 6^{dw} at 5o/	23.5
June 19	To mending a Borem Bottle	3.6		£24.15
1742			Balce Due Jacob Hurd	65. 3.6
Sep. 14	To mending a Snuff Box	4.		£89.18.6
1744				
March 7	To mending a Fan	6.		
1746				
Nov. 3	To 6 tea spoons & tongs 2^{oz}18^{dw}10^{grm} @ 5o/	7.5.		
	fashioning	5.0.0		
March 21	To 6 large Spoons 11^{oz} 17^{dw} @ 5o/	29.12.6		
	fashioning - - - 6	6		
1747				
May 1	To a pr Casters 7^{oz}11^{dw} - 5o/ - - - - - -	18.17.6		
	fashioning	12		
to	1 pare of Shew buckles	5 00		
		£89.18.6		
	To her part of one silver salver made for & given to Deacon John Phillips for Discharging his Trust of Executorship on ye Estate of Jo (? illegible)	26.13.4		
		£116.11.10		

NOTE: The entry about the salver above was made by another hand than Jacob's and was added after he made up the statement.

Jacob Hurd, Goldsmith

old silver amounted to approximately £3⅓ (23.25 divided by 7.)

When putting these figures into modern dollars, it must be remembered that no allowance is made for the differences in purchasing power between 1750 and 1939. With this reservation in mind, however, it may be of interest to reckon these costs in dollars. This may be done by using the ratio of six Massachusetts shillings to one dollar, the ratio set up by the Federal Government when the national currency was established. On this basis, the £3⅓ credit above mentioned would be worth about $11.00.

Now let us see how much the pair of casters weighing 7 ounces and 11 dwt. would have cost in dollars. At the given price of silver at 50 shillings an ounce, according to the bill, the materials cost £18–17–6 and the 'fashioning' £12–0–0, or 377.5 and 240 shillings, respectively. Dividing by 7 (to convert the paper money to its silver equivalence) and then dividing by 6 (to change silver shillings to dollars) these prices become approximately $9.00 for the silver and $5.70 for the labor. This total cost of $14.70 seems very low today, but in 1747 wages were lower and the purchasing power of the dollar was much greater.

By 1750 a decided change took place in Massachusetts money. The previous year the English Government had sent £185,000 sterling to the Province with orders to redeem the paper money. Accordingly a law was passed authorizing this redemption at the rate of one silver shilling for 7½ of the paper. By 1751 there was little paper money left outstanding, yet many merchants continued to reckon in terms of 'old tenor' up to the Revolution, always at the rate of 7½ old tenor for one of 'lawful money.'

Thus Nathaniel's bill for labor to Thomas Fayerweather (often quoted) is marked 'old tenor' in 1773 to the amount of £4–13–0. Dividing by 7.5, this amount is reduced to 12.4 shillings of lawful or silver money; and in turn this figure becomes $2.07 after dividing by 6, the ratio for Massachusetts money. This labor cost, while no doubt a fair one in 1773, seems low to us today, but again must be judged only in comparison with other contemporary prices.

[15]

Jacob Hurd, Goldsmith

To convert the values of old tenor, it is necessary to know the cost of an ounce of silver in paper-money shillings at the time in question, for which the following table is helpful.

	Paper shillings per ounce		Paper shillings per ounce
1700 to 1704	7	1734	25
1705 to 1710	8	1738	27
1714	9	1741	28
1716	10	1744	30
1719	12	1745	36
1721	13	1746	50
1723	15	1747	55
1726	16	1749	60
1730	20		

PLATE III

The Silver of Jacob Hurd

THE development of the style and designs of American silver has been traced in a number of books, and so well done, especially in Miss Avery's most valuable work entitled, *Early American Silver*, that being very generally understood, it will not be repeated here.

The New England goldsmiths of this period followed the Puritan style of the mother country, lagging a few years behind in point of time, as was natural, to allow changes in models to reach the colony.

It was the era of simplicity, particularly in Boston, and it was echoed in the silver which was produced. Both before and after Jacob's time, silver was more highly decorated. His predecessors, Dummer and Coney, while often producing pieces with little decoration, frequently used gadrooning and raised or cut decoration, and even after Jacob's day, when pieces became more graceful in form, they were embellished with engraved or repoussé ornamentation.

Jacob's style does not seem to have changed during his working life, which after all was less than forty years. In that short period during the eighteenth century, in a prim Puritan colony, there was not much chance of a change in style, even though the silversmiths of Boston followed from a distance those of England.

In looking over Jacob's pieces now extant, it is to be noted that he probably never made a flagon, for, as they were solely owned by churches, some would have survived. His porringers were invariably of the 'keyhole' type. Only one of his caudle cups is known today, and that is a very simple form made for the church in Reading, Massachusetts. Many of the older caudle cups were highly decorated, made for private use and later given to the church. They had gone out of fashion by Hurd's time, and it is doubtful if he ever made more than this one, which is dated 1744.

Curiously enough, only one seal made by Jacob Hurd has been found, and two by Nathaniel, and yet it can hardly be possible that Jacob and his sons made no more, and no doubt others will be found.

The seal made by Jacob in no way compares with that of the Mather arms cut by Nathaniel. Jacob's cutting is on silver, of armorial design and of poor workmanship. The design, if one can call it such, comprises a thin quatrefoil in the centre, with a surrounding circle of small rectangular crosses, and about eight curved, odd-shaped cuts around the crosses, and they in turn are enclosed by a series of small dots about the inner edge of the circular seal. The arrangement has little meaning and is of inferior execution, unworthy of such an experienced smith as Jacob.

The redeeming feature of the seal is the splendid boxwood handle three inches long, with excellent turnings, and a top two and three-eighths inches in diameter, which just fits the hand. The mark, as on Nathaniel's seal, is on the silver ferrule, and is No. 4 on the list.

The owner of this seal has some reason to believe that it was made for Sir Spencer Phipps, Lieutenant-Governor of Massachusetts, 1733–57, but proof of this has not been furnished. His dates, however, would render it possible, as he was born in 1684 and died in 1757.

We do not find any chocolate pots, spout cups, sweetmeat boxes, standing salts, or wine tasters among Jacob's 296 pieces now known, but, from loving cups and teapots to rings and thimbles, he seems to have made everything else.

There are among those catalogued, twenty-nine beakers and a similar number of cans, seventeen casters, twenty-one por- ringers, twenty-five tankards, twenty teapots, and forty-five spoons of different sizes; and also five rapiers. Curiously enough, though he must have made many buckles as the fashion then demanded, none have yet been found.

His beakers consist of two types, the plain flat bottom with an everted lip and the inverted bell shape standing on a cir- cular and moulded base.

His tankards are almost invariably of the same type, with a tapering body, a midband, a domed lid with various finials, and a handle with slight variations where it joins the body.

His teapots usually have a globular body, but in the grada- tion from the stiff straight spout to the fluted graceful swan's- neck one, and from the lid without hinge to the concealed hinge with engraved decoration, there is a marked improve- ment in design.

The large silver kettle on a stand with lamp is a remarkable one of graceful design, and his coffee-pots, of which we have found only three, are most charming.

His masterpieces are, however, the two great covered loving cups illustrated herein, pictures being better than any descrip- tion. An examination of these cups shows that they are almost identical and that they rely for their beauty upon their well- proportioned simplicity of line.

The story of these two cups and their owners will be of in-

Jacob Hurd, Goldsmith

terest to the reader. As for the Rowe cup, illustrated on Plate XIX, we cannot describe it better than to quote an account written by Mrs. Kathryn C. Buhler at the time of its acquisition by the Museum of Fine Arts in Boston:

> Made doubtless in the second quarter of the eighteenth century, its unusual size (H. 13½″, D. lip 6¾″, D. base 5:11/16″, Wt. 76 oz. 2 dwt.) gives further evidence of the wealth and grandeur of some of the households of colonial Boston.
>
> Its chief embellishment is a beautifully engraved cartouche and coat-of-arms; the latter, three paschal lambs, the crest a paschal lamb, was executed with a disregard of detail frequently found in armorial engravings by early American silversmiths, for it has no color indications. However, Dr. Harold Bowditch tells us that the Rowe families of Yorkshire and Devonshire used this design with a red field and white lambs in their coats-of-arms; and John Rowe, to whom this cup first belonged, was a son of the Devon family. He was born in Exeter, England, in 1715 and came to Boston at the age of twenty. His first business venture, apparently, was the purchase of a warehouse on Long Wharf in 1736; and for the next half century he was a prosperous merchant, ship and land owner, as well as a leading citizen of Boston. He kept a diary, parts of which survived and were published and in it we learn of his service on innumerable committees, and of entertainments attended and given by him.
>
> On several occasions he recorded the toasts drunk at a gathering, the numbers of them explaining perhaps the large size of this cup which was doubtless passed around at such festivities. Twenty-seven toasts were drunk at one occasion; and the persons and subjects most often in the lists, needless to say in the 1760s, were in the order of the toasts: 'The King,' 'The Queen & Royal Family'; sometimes 'The Parliament of Great Britain' and 'His Majesty's Ministry'; 'The Earl of Chatham,' 'Lord Chancellor,' and 'General Conway' appear always to have been included; then followed Earls, Dukes, and Officers by name; 'The Patrons of the British Colonies,' 'The Lords of the Admiralty,' 'The Army & Navy,' 'The United & Inseparable Interest of Great Britain and her Colonies,' 'May the True

[20]

PLATE IV

The Silver of Jacob Hurd

Interest of Great Britain and Her Colonies be Never Hidden of their Eyes,' more individuals, and then 'Prosperity of North America.' In the same decade 'wee Regulated the price of wine & punch... Twenty shillings a double Bowl Punch. Thirty shillings a Bottle Madeira.'

John Rowe was an active and interested member of Trinity Church, wherein he bought pew 82 in 1743 and served as a vestryman for many years. In 1743, also, he was married to Hannah Speakman, who appears throughout the diary under the formal address of 'Mrs. Rowe' or 'my dear Mrs. Rowe.' Her parents had been connected with Trinity Church from its beginning; and after John Rowe's death, his widow presented a cup to the Church, engraved with the Rowe arms and a crest of a stag's head.

He was a member of the House of Representatives in 1784, in which year the Journal of the House records:

'Mr. Rowe moved the House that leave be given to hang up the representation of a Cod Fish in the room where the House sits, as a memorial of the importance of the Cod-Fishery to the welfare of the Commonwealth as had been used formerly. The said motion having been seconded, the question was put, and leave given for the purpose aforesaid.'

In this he was prompted perhaps by his own enjoyment of a pastime frequently indulged in: 'we fished at Dedham Caufsway, had good sport,' 'went a fishing, had extraordinary sport,' 'wee set out after dinner for Spot Pond & fished there, we had but poor Sport. Wee caught ab° 4 dozen of small perch, a few pickerel & three Eylls.'

John Rowe left no children of his own; but in 1772 he had written: 'Oct. 19. After Dinner Capt Freeman Brought in my Kinsman Jack Rowe Son of my Brother Jacob of Quebeck. I am glad he is come. He is upwards of seven Year old'; and in a letter to his brother, 'he also handed mee your son Jack who is very well & a Merry Smart little fellow. I shall take care of him & Mrs. Rowe seems well pleased with him.' By the descendants of this lad the cup has been owned.

The Tyng cup, shown on Plate X, is more than an inch taller than the Rowe cup and weighs one hundred ounces, and the story of its purchase and presentation is an interesting one.

Edward Tyng (1683–1755), a grandson of that Edward who came to New England about 1630, was reared by his aunt, the wife of Governor Joseph Dudley. He married first a Miss Southack and, after her death in London in 1731, he married Anna Waldo, the daughter of a Boston merchant, and they had seven children.

When the war with France began, the Province owned an armed snow named *Prince of Orange* which had been commanded by the father of Tyng's first wife, Cyprian Southack. On his resignation, Tyng, who had been commissioned Captain by Governor Belcher in 1740, but had retired from the sea, was prevailed upon to succeed him and was given command. In 1745 he met and captured a French privateer which was lurking off the New England coast.

Besides the glory of the exploit, the capture was profitable to Captain Tyng, for by a recent law the value of the captured vessel became the property of the officers and crew, plus a bonus paid by the Province of £3 for each of the men on board the enemy privateer. This added £282 to the value of the vessel, and one-fourth the total was paid to Tyng as his share.

The Captain later commanded the frigate *Massachusetts*, carrying twenty-four guns, and was made commander of the fleet and fortifications of the Province. In 1745 he captured *The Vigilant*, a French man-of-war of sixty-four guns which he had decoyed and harried by several small vessels.

Shortly after, in 1748, Tyng retired again from the sea, dying some years later in 1755. The town of Tyngsboro was named for his family and incorporated in 1789.

The two accounts of the action between the *Prince of Orange* and the French privateer which appeared in the papers of the day are as follows:

[22   ]

The Silver of Jacob Hurd

THE BOSTON WEEKLY NEWS-LETTER

Friday, June 29, 1744

BOSTON

. . . .

On Monday last Capt. Tyng in the Province Snow, returned from a Cruize and brought in with him a French Privateer Sloop with 94 Men, mounted with 8 Carriage and 8 Swivel Guns, burthen between 70 and 80 Tuns, commanded by Capt. Delebroitz, which was fitted out from Cape Breton, and sail'd about 3 Weeks before: Capt. Tyng discover'd her last Saturday Morning about 9 o'Clock, as he was laying too off of Crabb-Ledge, 15 Leagues from Cape-Cod, it being very Calm. Perceiving she had a top-sail and was bearing down towards him, Capt. Tyng took her to be the Province Sloop commanded by Capt. Fletcher; but soon after, as she drew nearer, he suspected her to be a French Cruizer under English Colours, whereupon, in order to prevent a Discovery he ordered his Colours to be struck, his Guns to be drawn in and his Ports to be shut close, and at the same time the Bulk Heads to be taken down: When the Privateer had got within about Gun-shot of Capt. Tyng, taking the Snow to be a Merchant-Man, they fired upon him, upon which Capt. Tyng threw open his Ports, run out his Guns, hoisted his Colours and fired upon them: Perceiving their Mistake, they tack'd about, put out their Oars and tug'd hard to get off after firing two or three Guns more. It continuing very calm, Capt. Tyng was obliged to order out his Oars and to row after her, firing several Times his Bow Chase at her, in which the Gunner was so skilful, that 9 Times the Shot did some Damage either to her Hull or Rigging: About Two o'Clock the next morning he came up pretty close with them being very much guided by 4 Lanthorns which they had inadvertently hung out upon their Rigging in the Night; finding they were bro't to the last Tryal, attempted to board Capt. Tyng, which he perceiving, brought up his Vessel and gave them a Broad-Side, they having before thro' Fear all quitted the Deck. The Mast being disabled by a Shot, it soon after broke off in the middle: Upon firing this Broad-side they cry'd for Quarter; and then Capt. Tyng order'd

[23   ]

them to hoist out their Boat and bring the Captain on board, but they answer'd that their Tackling was so much shatter'd that they could not get out their Boat with it; they were then told they must do it by Hand: Accordingly they soon comply'd, and the Captain being brought on board deliver'd his Sword, Commission, &c. to Capt. Tyng, desiring that he and his Men might be kindly us'd, he was promis'd they should; and then the other Officers, being a 2d Captain, 3 Lieutenants, and others Inferiour, were brought on board, and the next Day the rest of the Men who were secur'd in the Hold.

The Night after Capt. Tyng brought them into this Harbour, they were convey'd ashore and committed to Prison here: and the next Morning 50 of them were guarded to the Prisons at Cambridge at Charlstown: The Officers and Men are treated with much Humanity and Kindnes.

'Tis remarkable that notwithstanding the great Number of Men on either Side, in the attack and surrender, there was not one kill'd or wounded.

BOSTON EVENING POST

Monday, July 2, 1744

Last Monday in the Afternoon, Capt. *Tyng* in our Province Snow *Prince of Orange*, arrived here from a short Cruize, and brought in with him a *French* Privateer Sloop of 8 Carriage and 10 or 12 Swivel Guns, with 94 Men, Capt. *Delabroitz* Commander, which he happily met with about 15 leagues from *Cape Cod*, about nine o'Clock on Saturday Morning, as he was coming in from Sea. The *Frenchman* taking him for an inward bound *Westindia* Man, (for he wisely kept his Guns housed) stood directly for him, and coming pretty near gave him a Gun which he returned with a Broadside; upon which the *Frenchmen* fired two Guns, then took to their Oars (there being but little Wind) and endeavoured to get away. This obliged Capt. *Tyng* to put out his Oars also, and after a hard Chace of 12 or 13 Hours, (during which Time Capt. *Tyng* treated his Men well with Liquor, and encouraged them all he could) he came up with the Sloop, and having given her a Broadside and a Volley of Small Arms, they cry'd for Quarters, but in their Panick forgot to

PLATE V

strike their colours, and kept them flying till some of our brave *English* Lads went on board, and exchang'd them for the King's Colours. Capt. *Tyng*'s Shot hapned to be so well placed, that the Sloop's Sails and Rigging were tore all to pieces; and when the *French* Captain came on board, he gave Capt. *Tyng* a great Character of his Gunner, saying, he was the best that ever he knew, for that every Shot he fired during the Chace, took Place, and did him some Damage in his Sails or Rigging. One Shot struck the Mast just below the Hounds, which so disabled it, that soon after they surrendered it broke off, and left the Sloop without an Inch of Sail or Rigging standing; so that Capt. *Tyng* was obliged to take her in Tow, or he could never have got her in. As the *French* fired but few Guns at Capt. *Tyng*, and as they all ran down in the Hold, when *he* was about to fire, it is not much to be wondered at that not a Man was kill'd or wounded on either Side.

The Prisoners were all landed in the Evening and conducted to Prison under a strong Guard, and in the Morning about 50 of them were removed to the Gaols in *Cambridge* and *Charlestown*. The Fellows are all as merry as they are ragged, and seem well pleased with their Circumstances, declaring, that they live better here than they did at Home, except five of the late Garrison at Canso, who entered voluntarily aboard the Privateer; and who are now sensible that they have been in a wrong Box.

The Privateer had been about 3 Weeks from Lewisburgh, and had plundered and destroyed the *English* Settlement at *St. Peter's* in *Newfoundland*, where they kill'd a great many Cattle, and carried off about 40 Sheep, several of which they had upon Deck when taken, and about 40 Barrels of the Beef in their Hold, but they had not taken any Vessel since they came upon this Coast: They could have taken several small ones, but did not care to be troubled with them; they wanted some rich Ships either inward or outward bound; and the Day before Capt. *Tyng* met with them, they had been within two Leagues of the Light House, and had their Eyes upon a Ship then in *Nantasket* Road, but were discouraged upon seeing a Vessel with a Pendant flying.

Jacob Hurd, Goldsmith

The Captain is Gentleman well known in Town, and has a Son at School about six Miles off. It is said he has been kind and serviceable to the *English* upon many Occasions at *Lewisburgh*, and he is now civilly treated himself, being at Liberty to walk about as he pleases.

It is allowed by all, both Friends and Enemies, that Capt. *Tyng* behaved with great Bravery and good Conduct during the whole Engagement and Pursuit; and the Town are so sensible of his Merit, and of the Importance of his Service to the Publick, that at an Adjournment of a Meeting of the Inhabitants on Tuesday last, they passed the following Vote, *viz.*

Upon a Motion made by Mr. Middlecot Cooke, *it was unanimously voted,* 'That the Thanks of the Town be given to Capt. *Edward Tyng*, Commander of the Province Snow, for the great Service he has done in taking and bringing into this Harbour, a *French* Provateer Sloop belonging to Cape *Britton*, mounting Eighteen Guns, and manned with 94 Men, commanded by Capt. *Delabroitz*, which has been cruising in our Bay for about three Weeks; and that the Select Men be desired to present the same to him accordingly.'

After Commodore Tyng died, the cup descended to his Loyalist son, Colonel William Tyng, and was taken from his house in Falmouth by country soldiery in 1775, but was later restored to the family by the Provincial Congress. It remained there among his descendants until purchased by Mr. Garvan, and presented to Yale together with an excellent portrait of Edward Tyng by an unknown hand. In it, he is dressed in a beautiful costume of the day, with a baton in his hand, a cocked hat under his arm, and wearing a flowing periwig. In the distance beyond a curtain is seen a square-rigged ship of war.

Jacob Hurd was an excellent engraver, though not as good as his son Nathaniel, but the embellishment on the Tyng cup, which was done when Nathaniel was but fourteen years old, could have been engraved by no one but Jacob himself. The

The Silver of Jacob Hurd

coat of arms on the Rowe cup, and that on several pieces of the Storer silver, are excellent. The trophies surrounding the Tyng inscription and the arrangement of the text, which contains several different kinds of letters, are well done, even though a modern engraver would probably space the words differently.

There can be no question about the reputation of Jacob, both as a silversmith and an engraver, and he will always stand among the first of our colonial craftsmen.

Regarding Jacob Hurd's silver marks, of which he had six, it was hoped that by comparing the pieces dated contemporaneously, excluding those pieces presented and dated after his death, some conclusion might be reached, so that undated silver might be ascribed to its proper period; but comparison of the marks and dates leaves us with no evidence of real value, as will be seen from the list below. To make matters more confusing, Jacob quite often put two different marks on the same piece.

Thus it would appear that when he or his craftsmen needed a punch, they took almost the first one at hand and used that. No. 1 with his full name thereon appears to have been used from 1721 when he was eighteen years old to the very last year of his life in 1758.

Catalogue of Silver Made by Jacob, Nathaniel, and Benjamin Hurd

THE list following comprises all the pieces made by the three Hurds which the writer has been able to find, though there undoubtedly must be others in existence which may appear from time to time.

Most of the pieces have been examined and measured by the author, and where that was not possible, by their owners. Photographs of all of the most important ones have been collected for study, and a number will be found herein as illustrations.

In the list the following symbols have been used, the measurements being given in inches:

H = Total height
D = Greatest diameter
DM = Diameter at mouth
DB = Diameter at Base
L = Length
W = Width
Wt = Weight

The marks of the maker corresponding to the numbers in the list will be found, for Jacob, on page 29, for Nathaniel on page 66, and for Benjamin on page 146.

[28]

PLATE VI

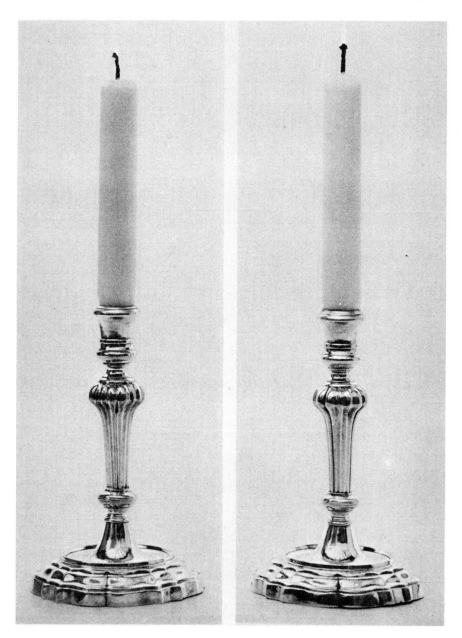

Silver Made by Jacob Hurd

1.  Full name, two lines, capitals and lower case. 1721-1758.

2. Initial and surname italic capitals, two sizes, in cartouche. 1727-1747.

3. Surname, italic capital and lower case in oval. 1729-1740.

4. Surname Roman capitals in oval. 1740-1756.

5. Same as No. 4 in larger size. 1750.

6. Surname, capital and lower case in cartouche. 1740-1750.

Facsimile of Jacob's signature on Rebecca Townsend's bill.

Engravings of inscriptions, coats of arms, and crests are indicated, and when known the names for the initials are given, as well as the name of the present owner when permitted.

References:

Where a piece has been mentioned or described in other publications, reference is made to the latter, and if possible to the page, as follows:

ACS = *American Church Silver*, published by the Boston Museum of Fine Arts in 1911.

AS = *American Silver*, published by the Boston Museum of Fine Arts in 1906.

B = Bolton's *American Armory*, 1927.

Garvan = Wherever this word appears, it refers to the Mabel Brady Garvan Collection, Gallery of Fine Arts, Yale University.

GFA = Bulletin of the Gallery of Fine Arts of Yale University.

HTC = *Harvard Tercentenary Catalogue*.

MFA = Records of the Boston Museum of Fine Arts.

MMA = Metropolitan Museum of Art, New York.

OSAC = *Old Silver of American Churches*, by E. Alfred Jones, 1913.

Silver Made by Jacob Hurd

1–2 *Alms Basins.* Pair of shallow circular dishes with wide rim: D, 13 3/8″; H, 2″; both marked # 2. Inscribed on rim of one in a scrolled panel, 'Dom⁵ Richardus Skinner, Euclesine isti Jesu/Christi apud Marblehead, cujus nuper Diacouns/fuit primorius, hoc Donum Taste mentorium/ Legarit Anno 1727.' Engraved on rim also, the Skinner coat of arms. Inscribed on rim of other, bought by church in 1728, 'Belonging to that Church of Christ in/Marblehead of wᶜʰ the Rev Mr Edward Holyoke is the Pastor.' ACS, p. 73; B, p. 151; OSAC, p. 267. Owner, Second Congregational Church of Marblehead.

3 *Baptismal Basin.* Deep circular dish with domed centre and wide rim. D, 13 3/8″; H, 3″; Wt, 27 oz. 3 dwt. Mark # 2. Byfield arms engraved on rim. ACS, p. 73; B, p. 27; OSAC, p. 33. Bequeathed by Nathaniel Byfield in 1723 to First Church of Boston, owner.

4 *Baptismal Basin.* Like above with moulded edge. Mark # 3. Inscribed: 'The Gift of Theo: Burrill Esq/to the first church of Christ in/Lynn.' Burrill arms engraved on rim. B, p. 26; ACS, p. 73; OSAC, p. 256. Owner, First Church of Lynn, Mass.

5 *Baptismal Basin.* Like above with domed centre. D, 13 1/8″; H, 3 1/2″. Mark # 2. On rim within two palm branches, 'The Gift of/Arthur-Savage Esqʳ/to Christ-Church/Boston 1732.' Engraved with Savage arms. B, p. 145; OSAC, p. 76. Owner, Christ Church, Boston.

6 *Baptismal Basin.* Like above with wide well. D, 12 1/2″; H, 2 1/2″. Mark # 4. On rim, 'The Gift of Mr John Hawes to the/first Church of Christ in Middletown/of which he is a member.' OSAC, p. 284. Owner, First Church of Christ, Middletown, Conn.

7–10 Beakers. Four, with wide body, curved lip, no base moulding. H, 4 1/4″; DM, 3 7/8″; DB, 3 1/8″. Mark # 6. Engraved on bottom, 'Hampton Old Church/1744.' ACS, p. 79; OSAC, p. 199. Owner, Congregational Church, Hampton, N.H.

Silver Made by Jacob Hurd

11 *Beaker.* Strait body, curved lip, moulding at base. H, 5 1/4"; DM, 3 3/4"; DB, 3 1/4"; Wt, 6 oz. 4 dwt. Mark # 2. Engraved, 'The Gift of/ N = Saltonstall and R = Cotton/to the first Church of Christ/in Woburn.' ACS, p. 76; OSAC, p. 504. Owner, First Congregational Church, Woburn, Mass.

12–15 *Beakers.* Four, like above. H, 4"; DM, 3 3/8"; DB, 2 3/4". Mark # 3. Engraved, 'The Gift of Dea^n/John Jacobs/to the 2^d Church/of Christ in/Hingham/1728.' ACS, p. 75; OSAC, p. 130. Owner, First Congregational Society, Cohasset, Mass.

16 *Beaker.* Like above. H, 5 5/8"; DM, 3 7/8"; DB, 3 3/8". Mark # 4. Engraved, 'The Gift of M^r =/Peter Emerson To/The first Church/of Christ in/Reading/1750.' OSAC, p. 475. Owner, First Congregational Church, Wakefield, Mass.

17 *Beaker.* Like above. H, 4 7/8"; DM, 3 7/8"; DB, 3 3/8". Mark # 4. Engraved 'The Gift/of Mr: John Pratt/To the first Church/in Reading/1746.' OSAC, p. 475. Owner, First Congregational Church, Wakefield, Mass.

18–19 *Beakers.* Two like above. H, 5 5/8"; DM, 4"; DB, 3 3/8". Mark # 6. Engraved, 'The Gift of Capt Thos Pool/to ye = 1st Church in Reading' (c. 1733). ACS, p. 78; OSAC, p. 474. Owner, First Congregational Church, Wakefield, Mass.

20 *Beaker.* Like above. H, 4 5/8"; DM, 3 3/4"; DB, 3 1/4". Mark # 4. Engraved in a circle, 'This Cup/was given to/The First Church/in Stratford by/ Leu^t Jos^h Beach/1746.' OSAC, p. 464. Owner, First Congregational Church, Stratford, Conn.

21 *Beaker.* Like above. H, 5"; DM, 3 5/8"; DB, 3 1/8". Mark # 6. Engraved, 'The Gift of/Mrs Mehetabel Fisher/to the First Church of Christ in/Braintree 1741.' ACS, p. 78; OSAC, p. 398. Owner, First Congregational Society, Quincy, Mass.

22 *Beaker.* Like above. H, 4 1/4"; DM, 3 3/8". Mark # 1 and # 6. Engraved, 'The Gift of Lieutenant/Samuell Stent to the/2^d Church In/Branford.' OSAC, p. 353. Owner, Congregational Church, North Branford, Conn.

23 *Beaker.* Like above. H, 5 5/8"; DM, 4"; DB, 3 5/8". Mark # 5. Engraved, 'The Gift/of the Rev^d/Mr Eb^{nr} Hancock/To the Church of/ Christ in/LEXINGTON' (c. 1749). ACS, p. 77; OSAC, p. 244. Owner, First Congregational Church, Lexington, Mass.

24 *Beaker.* Inverted bell-shaped body on low moulded base. H, 5 1/2"; DM, 3 7/8"; DB, 3 1/8". Mark # 2. Engraved, 'The Gift of/Mr WILLIAM CLAP/To the First Church/of Christ/in Dorchester/1745.' ACS, p. 71; OSAC, pp. 144, 145. Owner, First Church, Dorchester, Mass.

25 *Beaker.* Like above. H, 5 1/2"; DM, 3 3/4"; DB, 3 1/8". Mark # 6. Engraved, 'The Gift of/Mr Brice and Mrs Ann Blair/For the Use of

the presbyteria/Church in Long Lane, whereof/The Rev^d Mr Iohn Moorehead is/Pastor/in Gratitude to God for His Goodness to them and theirs in a Strange/Land BOSTON: May 1 1744 Set Deo Maxima Laus.' ACS, p. 79; OSAC, p. 78. Owner, Arlington Street Church, Boston.

26 *Beaker.* Like above. H, 5 1/2"; DM, 3 3/4"; DB, 2 3/4". Mark #4. Engraved, 'The Gift of/Lieu^t Eben Curtis/To the first Church/of Christ in/Stratford/1752.' OSAC, p. 464. Owner, Congregational Church, Stratford, Conn.

27 *Beaker.* Like above. H, 6"; DM, 4 1/4"; DB, 3 3/8". Mark #4. Engraved, 'The Gift of the Honble/Jsaac Lothrop Esqr/to the Third Church of/Christ in Plymouth/Sept ye 7 1743.' ACS, p. 78; OSAC, p. 375. Owner, First Parish, Plymouth, Mass.

28 *Beaker.* Like above. H, 6 1/4"; DM, 4 1/8"; DB, 3 1/8". Mark #3. Engraved in one line, 'The Gift of ye Honble Edmund Quincy Esqr to ye First Church in Braintree Feby 23 1737/8.' ACS, p. 75; OSAC, p. 397. Owner, First Congregational Society (Unitarian), Quincy, Mass.

29 *Beaker.* Like above. H, 5 1/2"; DM, 4"; DB, 3 1/2". Mark #6. Engraved, 'The Gift of/Deacon William Trowbridge/to/The Church of Christ/in/New Town/1744.' ACS, p. 79; OSAC, p. 324. Owner, First Church, Newton, Mass.

30–31 *Beakers.* Pair like above. H, 5 1/2"; DM, 3 7/8"; DB, 2 7/8". Mark #3. Engraved, 'The Gift of Theo. Burrill Esq/To the first Church of Christ in/Lynn.' The Burrill arms in centre of body. ACS, p. 75; B, p. 26; OSAC, p. 256. Owner, First Church, Lynn, Mass.

32 *Beaker.* Like above. H, 5 7/8"; DM, 4 1/8"; DB, 3 3/8"; Wt, 12 oz. 9^dwt. Mark #6. Engraved, 'The Gift of/Mrs. Hannah How/to the Church of Christ/on Church Green/BOSTON/In memory of her Husband/Mr Abr^m How. Dead/Feb 12 1740.' AS, p. 68; OSAC, p. 72. Owner, MFA by gift of New South Church, Boston.

33 *Beaker.* Like above. H, 5"; DM, 3 1/2"; DB, 2 3/4". Mark #1. Engraved, 'The gift of/Mr Ebenezer Clap/To the Church of/Milton/. ACS, p. 73: OSAC, p. 291. Owner, First Parish Congregational Church in Milton, Mass.

34 *Beaker.* Like above. H, 6 1/8"; DM, 4 1/4"; DB, 3 1/8". Mark #4. Engraved, 'The Gift of/Mr Peter Smith to/The First Church/in/Shrewsbury/AD : 1748.' ACS, p. 78; OSAC, p. 447. Owner, Congregational Church, Shrewsbury, Mass.

35 *Beaker.* Bell-shaped body with moulded lip and base. H, 5 5/8"; DM, 4"; DB, 3 1/8". Marks #1 and #4. Engraved in a fine cartouche, 'The Gift/OF Mr^s MARY WALKER Dec^d to the First/Church of Christ in Rehoboth/1747.' ACS, p. 76; OSAC, p. 163. Owner, Garvan.

36 *Bowl.* Hemispherical body with moulded rim on moulded base. D,

PLATE VII

Silver Made by Jacob Hurd

6 11/16″. Engraved (on one side), 'The Gift of Mr Jonas Rowlandson to Mr Thos. Woodbridge 1740.' (On the other), a ship under sail. ACS, p. 73. Owner, Edsel B. Ford, Esq., Detroit, Mich.

37 *Bowl.* Like above. D, 7 1/2″; H, 3 1/4″. Mark #4. Engraved, 'E/I * L.' ACS, p. 76. Owner, Mrs. G. L. Putnam (in 1911).

38 *Bowl.* Like above. H, 3″; D, 4″. Mark #3. Engraved with Dummer crest. See Bigelow Sale Catalogue #43.

39 *Bowl.* Like above. H, 2 5/8″; D, 5 7/8″; Wt, 7 oz. Mark #3. Engraved, 'Deborah Fraser/1738.' Owner, Mrs. Stephen C. Millet, New York.

40 *Bowl.* Curved sides with flaring foot. H, 3 1/2″; D, 6 3/8″. Mark #6. Engraved on side, 'E B Curtis,' and on bottom, 'M. W.' Bulletin of Detroit Institute of Arts #8. Owner, Detroit Institute of Arts, Detroit, Mich.

41 *Bowl.* For sugar. Engraved, 'H/R R' (for Robert and Ruth Hooper). Engraved with the Hooper arms. B, p. 83. Owner in 1927, Miss Currier, Newburyport, Mass.

42 *Bowl. Sugar Basin.* Inverted bell-shaped body on splayed moulded base, with saucer-shaped cover with reel handle. H, 3″; DM, 5 3/8″. Mark #3. Engraved in a scroll cartouche with Henchman arms. ACS, p. 74. Owner, Anonymous, Boston.

43 *Bowl.* Like above. H, 4 1/8″; Wt. 12 oz. 14 dwt. Mark #6. Engraved, 'Discrimine Salus/1745.' Arms of Trail, impaling Gale, on body. Crest of Trail, on cover. Owner, Mrs. Charles W. Whittlesey, New Haven, Conn.

44 *Bowl.* Like above. H, bowl 2 1/4″; H, cover 1 1/4″; DM, 4 1/4″; Wt, 9 oz. 5 dwt. Engraved, Henchman arms on body, Henchman crest on cover. Owner, Philip L. Spalding Estate, Boston.

45 *Bowl.* Like above. H, bowl 3 3/16″; H, cover 1 3/8″; DM, 5 13/16″; DB, 3 1/4″. Mark #4. Engraved, Henchman arms on body, Burrill crest on cover. Owner, Mrs. E. B. S. Callan, New York.

46 *Bowl.* Like above. H, bowl 2 7/8″; H, cover 2 5/8″; DM, 5 5/8″. Engraved, 'A W' (for Ann Wendell) and Wendell arms and crest. B, p. 177. Owner, Society for Preservation of New England Antiquities, Boston.

47 *Bowl.* Octagonal body on octagonal moulded base, moulded rim and turned finial. H, 4 3/8″. Mark #6. Engraved with Weld and Minot crests on panels. ACS, p. 71. Owner (in 1914), Miss Mary Allen.

48 *Bowl.* Like above, but with octagonal urn finial. H, 4 1/4″; D, 3 1/2″; L, 5″. Mark #2. Engraved, 'C,' inside cover, and a griffin's head crest. Owner, Mrs. F. P. Coffin, Schenectady, New York.

49-50 *Braziers.* A pair with pierced basins on three cabriole legs with hoofed feet, and three scroll supports above rim. Pierced bolted strainer. Turned wooden handle in silver socket. H, 3 1/2″; D, 6″; L, 12″. Mark #2. Owner, Garvan.

Silver Made by Jacob Hurd

51–52 *Braziers.* A pair of same design. D, 6 1/8″; L, 12 1/2″; H, 3 1/2″; Wt, 14 oz. 9 dwt. Mark # 2. Engraved on bottom, 'L H' (for Lydia Henchman). Henchman arms on body. AS, p. 66. Owner, Garvan.

53 *Brazier.* Like above. D, 6″; H, 3 1/4″; Wt, 17 oz. 15 dwt. Mark # 2. Engraved, 'J. H. to Mary C Shannon/1849,' and on bottom, '17^{oz} 15^d.' The Walker arms on body. Owner, Mrs. P. M. Hamlen, Boston.

54 *Brazier.* Like above. D, 6 1/16″. Mark # 2. Owner, Edsel B. Ford, Esq., Detroit, Mich.

55 *Brazier.* Like above. D, 6 1/4″; H, 3 1/4″. Mark # 3. Engraved with crest of 'a hound's head collared.' Owner, James B. Neale, Pennsylvania.

56 *Brazier.* Like above. D, 6 1/8″; H, 3 11/16″; L, 12 1/4″. Mark # 3. Engraved, 'L/B * M' and the Lynde crest. Owner, Robert Walcott, Esq., Cambridge, Mass.

57 *Brazier.* Like above. D, 6 5/8″; H, 4 1/16″; L, 13″. Mark # 4. Engraved, on bottom, 22–5–5. Owner, Philip L. Spalding Estate, Boston.

58–59 *Braziers.* A pair like above, but without sockets or handles. D, 6 1/8″; H, 3 1/4″. Engraved with Henchman arms on side and owned originally by Lydia Henchman. ACS, p. 73; B, p. 79. Owner, Garvan.

60 *Can.* An open drinking vessel, with pear-shaped body, reeded lip, turned and moulded base, with cast single scroll hollow handle. H, 4 3/8″; D, 3 1/2″; DM, 2 3/4″; DB, 2 7/8″; Wt, 9 oz. 8 dwt. Marks # 3 and # 1. Engraved, Pierce arms. B, p. 131; Lawton Sale Catalogue # 281. Owner, Detroit Institute of Arts.

61 *Can.* Mate to above. Owner, Joseph T. Pierce, Boston.

62–63 *Cans.* A pair. H, 4 3/4″; DM and DB, 3 1/8″. Mark # 3. Engraved with impaled arms of Mason and Williams; crest, a lion's head couped, and 'M/T * E' (probably for Thaddeus and Elizabeth (Sewall) Mason, m. 1748); also, '12^{oz}.–5^{dwt}.–o' on bottom. Owners, Mrs. Morgan Firth, New Haven, Connecticut, and Rev. Thaddeus Harris Winchester, Mass.

64–65 *Cans.* Pair like above. H, 5 5/8″; DM, 3 3/8″; DB, 3 3/4″; Wt, 14 oz. 3 dwt. Mark # 3. Engraved, 'The Gift of Deacon Ionathon Williams/ To the first Church in Boston/at his decease/March 27 1737'; Williams arms and crest. ACS, p. 75; B, p. 181; AS, p. 67; OSAC, p. 32. Owner, First Church, Boston.

66 *Can.* Like above. H, 5 1/2″; DM, 3 3/8″; DB, 3 3/8″. Mark # 3. Engraved, 'The Gift of/Mary Ingraham/to the Church in/Concord'; and on handle in earlier letters, 'B over N˙D to M over T:M' (Nathan Bond and wife to Tilly and Mary Merrick). ACS, p. 74; OSAC, p. 133. Owner, First Parish, Concord, Mass.

67 *Can.* Like above. H, 5 3/16″; DM, 3 1/4″. Mark # 4. Engraved, 'A Gift/from some of the/Principall Officers in the regiment/of Boston to/

Silver Made by Jacob Hurd

Mr Adjutant/Hunt/1747.' Surrounding the above is a later inscription, 'A Legacy left by Jabez Hunt to John Leverett jun^r 1763.' Owner, Hollis French, Esq., Boston.

68 *Can.* Like above. H, 5 1/4"; DM, 3 1/4"; DB, 3 1/4". Mark #6. Engraved, 'W/A + S' and 'S R S' on handle. Owner, George C. Gebelein, Esq., Boston.

69 *Can.* Like above. H, 4 1/2". Mark #2. Engraved, a crest with griffin. Owner, Mrs. Paul M. Hamlen, Boston.

70 *Can.* Like above. H, 4 15/16". Mark #3. Engraved, unknown arms, and with 'I H' in Roman caps on bottom. Owner, Edsel B. Ford, Esq., Detroit, Mich.

71 *Can.* Like above. H, 5"; Wt, 13 oz. 15 dwt. Engraved, 'I/D + S' and the Quincy arms. AS, p. 163. Owner, W. A. Jeffries, Esq., Boston.

72 *Can.* Like above. H, 4 3/4"; DM, 3"; DB, 3 1/4". Mark #2. Engraved, 'M + S' and the Simpson arms. Owner, Miss Marion Holyoke, New York.

73 *Can.* Like above. H, 4 7/8"; DM, 3 1/4". Mark #5. Engraved, Quincy and Conant arms impaled, and with 'I/D S.' Owner, Mrs. James H. Means, Boston.

74 *Can.* Like above. H, 5 1/8"; DM, 3 1/4"; DB, 3 3/8". Mark #3. Engraved, 'Sarah Bishop.' Owner, Mrs. Elaine Melchior, New York.

75 *Can.* Like above. H, 5". Mark #6. Engraved, 'G/S A' on handle, 'H I L' on body, and 'I/I F' on bottom, with the Gardiner (?) arms. Owner, MMA, New York.

76 *Can.* Like above. H, 5"; Wt, 12 oz. 11 dwt. 6 gr. Mark #6. Engraved, the Barrett arms, and 'S P' in script on front. Owner, MFA, Boston. (Tyler bequest.)

77 *Can.* Like above. H, 5 1/8"; Wt, 12 oz. 7 dwt. Mark #2. Engraved, 'I/I * S'. Owner, A. V. Stout, Esq., New York.

78 *Can.* Like above, but with body drop. H, 4 7/8"; DM, 3"; DB, 3 1/8"; Wt, 12 oz. 6 dwt. Mark #3. Engraved, 'M to T C.' Owner, Mrs. Thomas Hooker, New Haven, Conn.

79 *Can.* With similar body, but with double scroll handle, often with thumbrest of plain or acanthus design. H, 5"; DM, 3 1/16"; DB, 3 5/16". Mark #4. Engraved, with the Prescott arms. MMA records. Owner, A. B. A. Bradley, Esq., New York.

80 *Can.* Like above. H, 5 1/2"; DM, 3 1/2"; DB, 3 1/2". Mark #5. Engraved, the Barrett arms. Owner, Dr. John Homans, Boston.

81–82 *Cans.* A pair like above. H, 4 1/2"; Wts, 11 oz. 17 dwt., and 11 oz. 19 dwt. Mark #4. Engraved, the Vassall arms, and in script on bottom, 'Edmund Baker/1811.' ACS, p. 652; MFA records. Owner, Mrs. Mary E. Florance, Boston.

Silver Made by Jacob Hurd

83 *Can.* Like above. H, 5 1/8″. Mark #4. Engraved, 'W/D H' (for David and Hannah West), and also the West crest. ACS, p. 646. Owner, MFA, Boston.

84 *Can.* Like above. H, 5 3/8″; DM, 3 3/16″; DB, 3 1/4″. Mark #6. Engraved, the Lynde arms. Owner, MFA, Boston. (Lady Playfair bequest.)

85 *Can.* Standard body, but form of handle unknown. H, 5″. Mark #4. Engraved, coat of arms, with lion rampant, and on handle, 'L ▯ L.' Owner, Mrs. Paul Hamlen, Boston.

86 *Can.* Like above. H, 4 5/8″; Wt, 11 oz. 2 dwt. Mark #4. Engraved, the Chauncy arms. Owner, Mrs. F. S. Moseley, Boston.

87 *Can.* Like above. H, 5 1/2″; DM, 3 3/4″. Mark #5. Engraved, 'The Gift/of/Elizabeth Brooks/to the/First Church of Christ/in/Malden'; and on the handle 'M/D x E/1746.' OSAC, p. 258. Owner, First Church, Malden, Mass.

88 *Can.* With spout added. H, 5 1/8″. Mark #4. Engraved, the Quincy arms. Owner, Mrs. Josiah Quincy, Boston.

89-90 *Candlesticks.* Pair with turned sockets on reeded stem, with encircling band, resting on cone rising from splayed base with scalloped moulded rim. H, 6 1/4″. Mark #2. See *Antiques* of December, 1930. Owner, MMA, New York.

91 *Caster.* Octagonal body, moulded rim and base. Pierced cover with finial. Scroll handle. H, 4″; DB, 2″. Engraved, 'L H' on base (for Lydia Henchman, wife of Thomas Hancock, uncle of John). On front the Hancock crest, a demi-griffin. Owner, The Bostonian Society, Boston.

92 *Caster.* Like above. H, 4″. Mark #2. Engraved, 'C/A M' on bottom. Owner, Philip L. Spalding Estate, Boston.

93 *Caster.* Like above. H, 3 3/4″. Engraved, 'I/D L.' Owner, H. F. du Pont, Esq., Delaware.

94 *Caster.* Like above. H, 3 7/8″; DB, 2 1/8″. Mark #6. Engraved, 'The gift of Mrs J Ross/to H T 1743'/('H T' for Hannah Tricothek, b. 1724); and also 'I E C,' all on bottom. Owner, Hollis French, Esq., Boston.

95 *Caster.* Like above. H, 3 3/4″. Mark #3. Owner, Garvan.

96 *Caster.* Like above. H, 3 3/4″; DB, 2″. Mark #2. Engraved, 'Caleb & Martha Eddy/1747,' with 'M C' beside handle. Owner, Louis Joseph, Esq., Boston.

97 *Caster.* Like above. H, 4 3/4″; D, 1 7/8″. Mark #1. Engraved, 'L/ T L' on base. Owner, The Antique Galleries, Boston.

98 *Caster.* Like above. H, 4″; DB, 2″. Mark #5 twice. Engraved, '3-2-12,' scratched on bottom. Owner, Mrs. Andrew Payne, New Orleans, La. *Note.* A mate to this exists, but its location is unknown.

99 *Caster.* Cylindrical body with pierced top. Mark #2. Engraved, 'W/? C'

PLATE VIII

(for Comfort Weeks); other initial illegible. Owner in 1916, D. M. Prouty, Esq., Boston.

100–101 *Casters.* Pair, vase shape, with midband. H, 3 7/8''; and H, 3 1/2''. Mark #4. Engraved, 'D: Hewes.' With these casters are a pair of tripod salts (see #172–73). Owner, Mrs. Elizabeth Porter, Hartford, Conn.

102 *Caster.* Like above. H, 3 1/2''. Mark #4. Engraved, 'R/E R.' Owner, Hollis French, Esq., Boston.

103 *Caster.* Like above. H, 3 3/4''. Mark #4. Engraved in a circle on base, 'E. P./M F/M A Buzell.' ('E. P.' for Elizabeth Pepperell.) Owner, Garvan.

104 *Caster.* Urn shape with pierced steeple top and turned finial. H, 5''. Mark #4. Engraved, 'S x H.' (Clearwater Collection.) Owner, MMA. New York.

105 *Caster.* Like above. H, 5 1/4''. Mark #4. Engraved, 'S/I I' and 'I/I S.' OSAC, p. 653. Owner, Miss E. B. Brown (in 1911).

106–107 *Casters.* Pair of same design, but with star decoration below finials. H, 5 1/2''. Mark #4. Engraved, 'R T,' old capitals on base. Owner, P. Hammerslough, Esq., Hartford, Conn.

108 *Caster.* Like above without the decoration. H, 4 7/8''. Mark #4. Owner, Society for the Preservation of New England Antiquities, Boston.

109 *Chalice.* Inverted bell-shaped cup on high baluster stem, with splayed and moulded base. H, 8 3/8''; DM, 3 3/4''; DB, 3 5/8''. Mark #2. Engraved, 'A Gift to the/PRISBITERIAN CHURCH/in Long Lane/ Boston March yᵉ 1/1731.' ACS, p. 602; OSAC, p. 78. Owner, Arlington Street Church, Boston.

110 *Coffee Pot.* Tapered body, moulded base, cast spout with body drop, domed lid and knob finial, wooden handle. H, 10''; DB, 5 3/8''; Wt, 30 oz. Mark #4. Engraved, the Clarke arms and crest with swords reversed. Owner, H. F. du Pont, Esq., Delaware.

111 *Coffee Pot.* Like above. H, 9 1/4''; DM, 3''; DB, 4 3/4''. Mark #2. Engraved, crest a unicorn's head. Owner, Garvan.

112 *Coffee Pot.* Like above. H, 9''; Wt, 28 oz. 17 dwt. Mark #4. Engraved, the Alleyne arms. AS, p. 158; ACS, p. 649; B, p. 3. Owner, Garvan.

113 *Cream Jug.* Pear-shaped body, three slipper feet, serrated rim, double scroll handle. H, 4''. Marked twice #4. Body decorated with three trifid arched frames with scenes showing swans in pond; Castle William, Boston; house and trees. Engraved, 'M ι E' on base. Owner, Garvan.

114 *Cream Jug.* Like above. H, 4''; Wt, 3 oz. 5 dwt. Mark #4. On side panels, house and ship; and house and trees; on front panel, the arms of Benjamin Johnson of Marblehead. AS, p. 161. Owner, Garvan.

115 *Cream Jug.* Like above. H, 3 7/8''; Wt, 3 oz. 18 dwt. Mark #4. On side

[37]

panels, landscape with trees; and marine view with ships. In front panel, the Vassall arms. Engraved, 'E C P' on bottom. Owner, Hollis French, Esq., Boston.

116 *Cream Jug.* Pear-shaped body, serrated rim, three bandy legs with three-toed feet and double scroll handle. H, 3 3/4"; D, 2 7/8". Engraved, 'The Gift/G Russell to/his grand daughter/Eliz:Trivet/1749.' Elizabeth Trivet, b. 1744, d. 1825, m. 1st, Th. Wendell; 2d, Saml. Hooper. Owner, S. H. Hooper, Esq., Boston.

117 *Cream Jug.* Can shape, with nose and double scroll handle. H, 3 1/2"; D, 2"; DB, 2". Mark # 3. Engraved on bottom, 'B/P E.' Owner, Hollis French, Esq., Boston.

118 *Cream Jug.* Like above. H, 3 1/2"; DB, 2"; DM, 2". Mark # 3. Engraved, 'W E H,' in old script above a crest of a column on a torse. ACS, p. 627. Owner, Hollis French, Esq., Boston.

119 *Cream Jug.* Like above, but with loose domed moulded cover with finial. H, 3 1/4"; D, 2 1/4", for body, and H, 1 1/4", D, 1 3/4", for cover. Mark # 6. Engraved, 'L/N M' on handle, and 'L' on cover bezel. (Hurd mote spoon found in this jug, see later.) Owner, Hollis French, Esq., Boston.

120 *Cream Jug.* Pear-shaped body, long lip, scalloped rim, S handle. Body decorated in repoussé with medallion, on circular base. H, 4"; DB, 2". Mark # 4. Engraved, 'T M P,' script monogram. Owner, Miss Ethel C. Lenssen, New York.

121 *Cup for Caudle.* Plain gourd-shaped body on low base, with two solid cast scroll handles. H, 3 1/2"; DB, 3"; DM, 3 7/8". Engraved in double circle, 'The Gift/of/Capt Joseph Burnap/to yᵉ First Church in/ Reading.' ACS, p. 657; OSAC, p. 474. (Only caudle cup by Hurd so far found, the donor bequeathing money for a 'vessell' in 1744.) Owner, First Congregational Church, Wakefield, Mass.

122 *Cup.* For a child. H, 3 1/2"; DM, 3 1/4". Mark # 6. Engraved, crest, a deer. Owner, Mrs. Paul Hamlen, Boston.

123 *Cup,* with cover. For a child. H, 3 1/8"; H, with cover, 4 1/2". Mark on body and cover, # 4. Engraved, the Hooper arms. Owner, Mrs. Paul Hamlen, Boston.

124 *Cup.* For a child. Small body, beaker shape, with flaring lip and base moulding, with S-shape moulded strap handle. H, 2 3/4"; DM, 2 7/8"; DB, 2 1/8". Mark # 3. Owned by private collector.

125 *Cup.* For Communion. Deep bell body on low moulded base with two solid moulded S-shape handles. H, 7"; DM, 4 7/8"; DB, 3 1/4"; Wt, 17 oz. 2 dwt. Mark # 6. AS, p. 68; ACS, p. 79; OSAC, p. 36. Owner, Second Church, Boston.

126-127 *Cups.* Pair like above for Communion. H, 5 7/8"; DM, 4 1/4"; DB, 3 1/8". Mark # 6. Engraved, 'The Gift of Mr Francis/Leath to the

[38   ]

Ch^h of/Christ in Medford/1742.' ACS, p. 79; OSAC, p. 273. Owner, First Parish, Medford, Mass.

128 *Cup.* For Communion. Beaker-shaped body with flaring lip, bottom moulding, and two ribbed strap handles. H, 4 7/8"; DM, 3 3/4"; DB, 3 1/8". Mark #2. Engraved, 'The Gift/of Mr Ichabod Alis/to the Church In/Hatfield/1747.' (Donor b. 1675, d. 1747.) ACS, p. 72; OSAC, p. 212. Owner, Garvan.

129 *Cup.* Loving cup with bell-shaped body on substantial moulded base, with moulded midband. Two cast single scroll handles. High loose moulded cover and turned finial. Known as the Rowe Cup (see text). H, 13 1/2"; DM, 6 3/4"; DB, 5 11/16"; Wt, 76 oz. 2 dwt. Marks #2 and #4. Engraved above the midband in an embellished cartouche are the Rowe coat of arms and crest. ACS, p. 71; MFA Bulletin #34, p. 104. Owner, MFA, Boston.

130 *Cup.* Loving cup of similar design to above, but larger. Known as the Tyng Cup (see text). H, 15 1/8"; Wt, 100 oz. Marks #1 on base, #4 on cover. Engraved in a trophy of arms and flags is the following inscription: 'To/Edward Tyng Esqr/Commander of ye Snow/"Prince of Orange"/As an acknowledgement of/his good Service done the/TRADE in taking ye First/French Privateer/on this coast/the 24th of June/1744 This plate is presented/By Several of ye Merch^{ts}/in Boston New/England.' ACS, p. 276; GFA Bulletin #206, p. 105. Owner, Garvan.

131 *Dish.* Shallow bowl with fluted rim, chasing between flutes. H, 1 3/4"; D, 8 1/2". Mark #3. No engraving. Owner, James B. Neale, Esq., Pennsylvania.

132 *Jug.* Covered wine flask with curved handle. H, 13". Made for a Hurd descendant, Nathaniel Curtis (b. 1740), at time of his wedding to his cousin, Hannah Curtis. Owner, Mrs. H. E. Curtis, Wis.

133 *Kettle on stand.* Spherical body with flanged base and many-sided spout. Lid with ivory finial. Hinged bail on body, which rests on graceful stand of four curved legs with claw feet. Lamp support between legs. Total H, 14 3/8"; H, 9 1/8". Marks #1 on bottom and #3 on cover. Engraved, Lowell arms quartering Leversedge, with ornaments. ACS, p. 75; B, p. 105. Owned by a private collector.

134 *Ladle.* For punch. Scalloped and ribbed bowl with curved and forked silver socket and turned wooden handle. Bowl 3 5/8" x 2 1/4"; H, 1"; socket, 3 1/2"; handle, 7 1/4". Mark #4. Engraved, 'N/I * M.' Owner, George Stevens, Esq., Narragansett, R.I.

135 *Ladle.* For punch. L, 12 1/2". Mark #4. Engraved, 'H E.' Owner, MFA, Boston.

136–137 *Links.* Gold links for cuffs. Pair of two octagonal plates, with engraved borders, medallions in centre with link between. Mark #4. Scratched on back, 'I D.' Owner, Wadsworth Athenaeum, Hartford, Conn.

[39   ]

Silver Made by Jacob Hurd

138 *Mace.* Silver oar blade with socket at end of short loom to attach wood wand when using as mace in the Admiralty Court of the Province. L, 23 1/2″. Mark # 5. Engraved, on one side, the royal arms of England between the initials 'G' and 'R'; on other side, a foul anchor. See *Boston Bar Bulletin* of December 14, '31. Owner, Massachusetts Historical Society, Boston.

139–140 *Mugs.* Pair, tankard-shaped body with mouldings at rim, midband, and base, with hollow single scroll handle. H, 4 3/4″. Mark # 2. Engraved, 'Samuel Whitney/Castine' and 'W/1793.' ACS, p. 72. Owners, J. C. and E. P. Whitney, Boston (in 1911).

141 *Mug.* Like above. H, 5 9/16″; DM, 4 1/4″; DB, 5 3/16″. Marked # 2 twice. Engraved, Dudley arms of lion rampant with lion's head crest. MMA records. Owner, J. P. Marquand, New York.

142 *Mug.* Like above. H, 4 3/4″; DM, 3″; DB, 3 1/2″. Marked twice # 2. Engraved, 'G/I L.' Owner, Philip L. Spalding Estate, Boston.

143 *Mug.* Like above. Mark # 3. Engraved, 'P/C M' (for Cabot and Mary Parker). Owner, MFA, Boston.

144 *Pap Boat.* Shallow bowl with long nose. L, 5 3/4″; D, 2 3/4″; H, 1 3/8″. Mark # 4. Engraved, for John and Mary Channing (m. 1746), 'C/I * M/to/M C.' Owner, Mrs. William R. Wistar, Philadelphia.

145 *Patch Box.* Shallow oval decorated box. L, 1 7/16″; W, 1 1/8″; H, 5/16″. Mark # 2. Engraved, the Coombs crest. Owner, W. M. Jeffords, Pennsylvania.

146 *Paten.* Circular plate with moulded edge and reel handle below. H, 2 1/8″; D, 6 5/8″. Mark # 3. Engraved, the Dawes arms. ACS, p. 74. Owner, MFA, Boston.

147 *Porringer.* Shallow circular bowl with rounded sides and bottom. Cast handle at rim in perforated keyhole pattern. D, 5 3/8″; H, 1 3/4″; Wt, 5 oz. 6 dwt. 8 gr. Mark # 4. Engraved, on front, 'M A Bowditch'; on bottom, 'Harold Bowditch/from J. Marcou.' Engraved on handle, crest, a mailed arm with naked fist grasping a stag's antler. Owner, Dr. Harold Bowditch, Boston.

NOTE. All following porringers are of same design as above.

48 *Porringer.* D, 5 7/16″. Mark # 2. Engraved, 'C/M * M.' Owner, Edsel B. Ford, Esq., Detroit, Mich.

149 *Porringer.* Owner, Edsel B. Ford, Esq., Detroit, Mich.

150 *Porringer.* D, 5 5/8″; H, 1 3/4″; Wt, 8 oz. 15 dwt. Mark # 2. Engraved, 'T C' on front of handle, and on back, 'Temperence Clap/1740.' Owner, Mrs. H. Norris Harrison, Rydal, Penn.

151 *Porringer.* Marks # 1 and 2. Engraved, 'D F' (for David Flynt); 'M I' (for Mary Jackson); 'S W' (for Sarah Wendell); 'O W H' (for Oliver

PLATE IX

Silver Made by Jacob Hurd

Wendell Holmes, Sr.), and 'O W H' (for Oliver Wendell Holmes, Jr.). Owner, Edward J. Holmes, Esq., Boston.

152 *Porringer.* D, 5". Mark # 6. Engraved, 'H S F' (for Harriet S. Fuller of Norwich). Owner, Miss S. C. Hyde, Norwich, Conn.

153. *Porringer.* D, 5"; H, 1 7/8", L of handle, 2 3/4". Mark # 4. Engraved, 'C J M' in cipher. AS, p. 69. Owner, Garvan.

154 *Porringer.* D, 4". Mark # 3. Engraved, 'H — H,' on handle. Owner, Garvan.

155 *Porringer.* D, 4 7/8"; H, 2". Mark # 2. Engraved, 'A B,' in old script monogram. Owner, George C. Gebelein, Esq., Boston.

156 *Porringer.* D, 5 1/8"; H, 1 3/4". Mark # 1. Engraved, 'B/T * M' (for Thomas and Margaret Binney). Owner, George C. Gebelein, Esq., Boston.

157 *Porringer.* D, 5"; H, 1 3/4". Mark # 2. Engraved, 'B/S * D.' Owner W. M. Jeffords, Pennsylvania.

158 *Porringer.* D, 5"; H, 1 3/4". Mark # 1. Engraved, 'J L to M E L.' Owner, Mrs. Breckenridge Long, Laurel, Md.

159 *Porringer.* D, 5 1/8"; H, 1 3/4". Mark # 4. Engraved, 'P/I * S.' Owner, Mrs. J. E. Marble, South Pasadena, Cal.

160 *Porringer.* D, 5 3/16". Mark # 6. Engraved on handle, 'C/S T/to /R L,' and on bottom, '1767.' Owner, Elizabeth Warren Mueller, New York.

161 *Porringer.* Mark # 1. Engraved, 'The gift of Henry Flynt Esq/to Hannah Sprague 1758,' and the Flynt crest. HTC, p. 38. Owner, Philip L. Spalding Estate, Boston.

162 *Porringer.* D, 5"; DB, 5 1/4"; H, 2". Marked twice # 4. Engraved (late letters), 'E.S. 1771' (for Elizh Salisbury), and 'S B S 1831' (for Saml B. Sumner). Owner, H. B. Sumner, Esq., Lakeville, Mass.

163 *Porringer.* D, 5 1/8". Mark # 2. Engraved, 'B' (for Baker). ACS, p. 71. Owner, Ray Baker Taft, Esq., Boston.

164 *Porringer.* D, 5 1/4"; H, 1 3/4"; Wt, 7 oz. Engraved, 'W/T * ?' Owner, Victor A. Watson, Esq., London, Eng.

165 *Porringer.* D, 5"; Wt, 7 oz. 7 dwt. Marks # 2 and # 1. Engraved, 'S H.' AS, p. 66. Mrs. Miles White Sale Catalogue # 465.

166 *Porringer.* D, 5 1/8"; H, 2 3/4". Engraved, 'R/S · M.' Owner, Irving W. Davis, Esq., Danielson, Conn.

167 *Porringer.* Keyhole type. In South Kensington Museum, London. Owner, Victor A. Watson, London, Eng.

168 *Rapier.* Silver hilt with spherical pommel and finial, wooden grip wound with silver wire. Single curved quillon and hand guard with two open knuckle bows, and plain oval 'pas d'âne.' Three-cornered blade with silver-mounted leather scabbard. L, 37 3/4". Mark # 3. ACS, p. 78. Owner, Dwight Blaney, Esq., Boston.

169 *Rapier*. Like above. L, 37″. Mark #3. Engraved, 'R H 1735' (for Colonel Richard Hazen). On scabbard band, 'Cost £13 15 9.' See *Antiques*, March, 1930. Owner, Joseph D. Little, Esq., New York.

170 *Rapier*. Like above. L, 37″. Mark #1. Engraved, 'Lieut. Samuel Clarke 1752.' owned by private collector.

171 *Rapier*. Like above. L, 38 1/4″. Mark #4. Original owner, General John Winslow. Present owner, Pilgrim Society, Plymouth, Mass.

172 *Rapier*. Like above. L, 35″. Mark #4. Engraved, 'I. L. Bracket.' Owner, Portsmouth Historical Society, Portsmouth, N.H.

173 *Ring*. Gold mourning ring, plain band of semicircular section. Mark #3. Engraved on inside, 'E D Obt 13″ Sept. 1740 AE 36.' Owner, Essex Institute, Salem, Mass.

174–175 *Salts*. Pair of trencher type with moulded and splayed sides, long octagon shape with oval cellars on top. L, at base, 2 7/8″, at top, 2 3/8″, Wt, 2 oz. 6 dwt. each. Mark #4 on each. Walpole Note Book, February, '37. Owner, Hollis French, Esq., Boston.

176–177 *Salts*. Pair of circular tripod salts with bandy legs and turtle feet. These accompanied the vase pepper casters #97, 98. H, 1 7/8″; D, 2 1/2″. Mark #4. Engraved, 'D: Hewes' on bottom, with a deer's crest on body. Owner, Miss E. Q. Porter, Hartford, Conn.

178 *Salt*. Circular body, moulded rim, on three bandy legs. D, 2 3/4″. Mark #4. Owner, heirs of Mrs. Richard Morgan, Plymouth, Mass.

179 *Sauce Boat*. Wide oval bowl, flaring mouth, scalloped rim, three curved legs, duck feet, and open scroll handle. L, 8″; H, 3″; Wt, 12 oz. Mark #5. Engraved, 'P/T * S.' Owned by private collector.

180 *Sauce Boat*. Like above. L, 8″; H, 3″; H, to handle top, 4 1/2″; Wt, 12 oz. Mark #4. Engraved, on bottom, 'The pair 27ᵒᶻ 17ᵈʷ.' Crest, a crowned lion's head. Owner, Garvan.

181 *Sauce Boat*. Like above. L, 7 1/2″; W, 4″; H, to top of handle, 4″. Mark #4. Engraved, the Walcott arms. B, p. 172. Owner, Hon. Robert Walcott, Cambridge, Mass.

182 *Saucepan*. Circular in horizontal section, oval in vertical, with silver socket and turned wooden handle. Two incised lines below rim. H, 3 1/2″; DM, 3 3/4″. Marks #1 and #3. Engraved, 'P D.' Owner, Mrs. James H. Means, Boston.

183 *Seal*. Silver seal and socket with boxwood handle. D seal, 1″; L seal, 1 1/16″; D socket, 13/16″. Mark #4. Owner, George R. Harlow, Esq., Cleveland, Ohio.

184. *Snuff Box*. Elliptical body, moulded rim, and convex cover. L, 3″; W, 2 1/8″, Wt, 10 oz. 8 dwt. Mark #2. Engraved, 'Ioseph Burbeen/1729' (Burbeen was Harvard 1731.) Owner, Garvan.

Silver Made by Jacob Hurd

185 *Snuff Box.* L, 3 1/4". Mark # 4. Engraved, 'G * L.' Unknown crest on cover. Owner, Clapp and Graham, New York.

186 *Snuff Box.* Oval gold body and hinged lid. L, 2 5/8"; W, 2". Mark # 3. Engraved, arms of Lieutenant-Governor Dummer on cover. OSAC, p. 36. Owner, Nathaniel Hamlen Estate, Boston.

187 *Spoon, Serving.* Large oval bowl with rat tail. Long octagon tapering handle with two encircling bands, moulded tip with finial. L, 16 1/2". Mark # 3. Engraved, 'S/W K'/ and a crest of a bird rising. (Clearwater Collection.) Owner, MMA, New York.

188 *Spoon, Serving.* Long deep bowl with double drop. L, 15". Mark # 1. Engraved, crest of boar's head pierced by arrow, with 'E H' below. Owner, Mrs. J. E. Marble, South Pasadena, Cal.

189 *Spoon, Serving.* Large bowl with long handle. L, 15"; bowl, L, 4 3/4"; W, 2 3/4". Mark # 2. Engraved, the Mascarene crest. Owner, Nathaniel Hamlen Estate, Boston.

190 *Spoon, Serving.* Large bowl, double drop, with long handle and rib front end. L, 11 1/2"; bowl, L, 3 3/4". Mark # 2. Engraved, crest, a griffin passant on a torse. Owner, Mrs. J. D. Barney, Boston.

191 *Spoon.* Late trifid with rat tail. L, 8". Mark # 2. Engraved, 'A. W.' Owner, Mrs. Paul M. Hamlen, Boston.

192 *Spoon.* Rat tail, rib end. L, 7 7/8". Mark # 2. Engraved, 'M * B,' old capitals, and 'M * S.' Owner, George C. Gebelein, Esq., Boston.

193 *Spoon.* Like above. L, 7 5/8". Mark # 2. Engraved, 'S * H.' Owner, Charles Montgomery, Wallingford, Conn.

194 *Spoon.* Like above. L, 7 5/8". Mark # 2. Engraved, 'N = S = C' (New South Church). AS, p. 67; ACS, p. 72; OSAC, p. 73. Owner, MFA, Boston. Gift of the Church.

195 *Spoon.* Like above. L, 7 5/8". Mark # 2. Engraved, 'K/E L.' Owner, MMA, New York.

196 *Spoon.* Like above. L, 7 1/2". Mark # 2. Engraved, 'D:G/to/R C' (Reading Church). ACS, p. 71; OSAC, p. 476. Owner, First Congregational Church, Wakefield, Mass.

197 *Spoon.* Like above. L, 8". Mark # 2. Engraved, demi-griffin on a torse, with 'M I born 1774.' Owner, Mrs. H. F. Clarke, Boston.

198 *Spoon.* Like above. L, 7 1/4". Mark # 2. Engraved, 'T/E ‖ E.' Owner, George C. Gebelein, Esq., Boston.

199–204 *Spoons.* Six with double drop and rib end. L, 8 1/4". Mark # 2. Engraved, 'N/I * M.' Owners, (1) I. W. Davis; (2) H. T. Bannon; (3) George C. Gebelein.

205–208 *Spoons.* Four same as above. L, 8". Mark # 2. Engraved, 'B/I = D.' Owner, George C. Gebelein, Esq., Boston.

209 *Spoon.* Like above. L, 7 5/8″. Mark #6. Engraved, 'W/I M.' Owner, S. W. Smith, Esq., Boston.

210 *Spoon.* Like above. L, 8″. Mark #2. Engraved, 'Q/I H' (Josiah and Hannah Quincy). ACS, p. 72. Owner, MFA, Boston.

211 *Spoon.* Like above. L, 8″. Mark #2. Engraved, 'Joshua Green.' ACS, p. 72. Owner, MFA, Boston.

212 *Spoon.* Like above. L, 7 3/4″. Mark #2. Engraved, 'S/D * I.' Owner, Garvan.

213 *Spoon.* Like above. L, 8″. Mark #2. Engraved, 'S H.' Owner, Rudolf P. Pauly, Esq., Boston.

214 *Spoon.* Like above. L, 7 7/8″. Mark #2. Engraved, 'D.T/to/D.Webb/ born Feb 26/1735/6.' Owner, unknown.

215 *Spoon.* Like above. L, 8 1/16″. Mark #2. Engraved, 'A C.' Owner, Stanley Inneson, Esq., New York.

216 *Spoon.* Like above. L, 7 11/16″; Wt, 1 oz. 15 dwt. 2 gr. Mark #2. Engraved, 'BW to DW' (BW for Benjamin Wadsworth, eighth Harvard President). HTC, #138. Owner, Harvard College.

217 *Spoon.* With drop and buckle on bowl. L, 7 3/4″. Mark #2. Engraved, 'K/B ı D.' Owner, Miss Ethel C. Lenssen, New York.

218 *Spoon.* Single drop, rib front and pierced bowl for straining. L, 8 1/2″. Mark #2. Engraved, 'W/K A.' Pierced on bowl are initials 'I A.' (Karolik Collection.) Owner, MFA, Boston.

219 *Spoon.* No data obtainable, but mentioned in Diary of Samuel Sewall as given by him to his grandchild. (See text.)

220 *Spoon.* Single drop and shell on bowl, rib end. L, 4″. Mark #3. Engraved, 'P T/to/D W.' Owner, Hollis French, Esq., Boston.

221 *Spoon.* Like above. L, 4 1/2″. Mark #4. Engraved, 'H:E.' Owner, George C. Gebelein, Esq., Boston.

222 *Spoon.* Like above. L, 4 1/2″. Mark #4. Engraved, 'M L/1756.' Owner, Pilgrim Society, Plymouth, Mass.

223–224 *Spoons.* Pair like above. L, 4 1/2″. Mark #6. Engraved with a ship. AS, p. 66. Owner, Mrs. C. W. Lord, in 1906.

225–226 *Spoons.* Pair like above. L, 4 1/2″. Mark #3. ACS, p. 78. Owners, MFA and Mass. Hist. Soc., Boston.

227–228 *Spoons.* Pair with rayed shell on bowl, rib end. L, 4 9/16″. Mark #4. Engraved, 'I/I = M.' Owner, Garvan.

229 *Spoon.* Like above. L, 4 15/16″. Mark #4. Engraved, 'E ı P.' Owner, Dr. George B. Cutten, Hamilton, N.Y.

230 *Spoon.* Like above. L, 4 5/8″. Engraved, 'M·Y.' Mark #4. Owner, Dr. George B. Cutten, Hamilton, N.Y.

PLATE X

Silver Made by Jacob Hurd

231 *Spoon.* Like above. L, 4 7/16". Mark #2. Engraved, 'P .ˑ. M.' Owner, Dr. George B. Cutten, Hamilton, N.Y.

232 *Spoon.* Mote, with pierced bowl and pointed stem. L, 5 1/8". Mark #4. Engraved on back of bowl, 'M C'; inside bowl, '1740.' This piece belonged with the covered cream jug by J. Hurd listed. Owner, Hollis French, Esq., Boston.

233–234 *Spoons.* Pair of shovel salt spoons. L, 3". Mark #4. Engraved, 'C I/to/ TEW.' Owners, T. B. Coolidge *et al.*, Boston.

235 *Strainer.* Perforated bowl and double handle. L, 10 5/8". Mark #4. Owner, Edsel B. Ford, Esq., Detroit, Mich.

236 *Strainer.* Like above. L, 11 3/8"; D, 3 15/16". Mark #4. Owner, Miss M. Furness, Chicago.

237 *Sugar Scissors.* With cutting edge, shell ends and decoration. L, 4 1/4". Mark #4. In private collection.

238 *Sugar Scissors.* Like above. L, 4 3/4". Mark #4. Engraved, 'N L.' ACS, p. 76. Owner, Hollis French, Esq., Boston.

239 *Sugar Scissors.* Like above. L, 4 3/8". Mark #4. Engraved with griffin's head crest. Owner, Hollis French, Esq., Boston.

240 *Sugar Tongs.* L, 5 3/4"; W, 3/8". Mark #4. Engraved, 'V/A ıı D.' Owner, Miss Ethel C. Lenssen, New York.

TANKARDS. All of Jacob Hurd's tankards are of nearly identical design, only being changed in some small detail, therefore it is to be understood that the description of the first tankard, below listed, will apply to all except where otherwise noted.

241 *Tankard.* Tapered body with midband, moulded lip and base, domed and moulded lid, turned finial, scroll purchase, S handle with oval boss at tip. H, 7 1/4"; Wt, 22 oz. 9 dwt. Mark #3. Engraved, 'The Gift of Elijah Danforth Esqʳ/To the Church in Dorchester/Anno Domini 1736.' Above the midband, the Danforth arms. AS, p. 157; B, p. 45; OSAC, p. 147. Owner, First Church, Dorchester, Mass.

242 *Tankard.* H, 7 3/4"; DM, 4"; DB, 5 1/8"; Wt, 25 oz. Mark #5. Engraved, 'The Gift of Deacon/Hopestill Clap to the Church/of Christ in Dorchester/1748.' Above the midband, the Rogers arms. AS, p. 68; ACS, p. 75; B, p. 141; OSAC, p. 148. Owner, as above.

243 *Tankard.* With acorn finial. Mark #4. Engraved above the midband, a snow under full sail; below the band, 'The John and Ann/John Sprout to the 2d/Presbyterian Church Phᵃ/1795.' On bottom, 'Snow/I & A.' On handle, 'S/I * S' (for James and Sarah Sprout). Owner, Second Presbyterian Church, Philadelphia.

244 *Tankard.* H, 7 3/4"; DM, 4 1/8"; DB, 5". Marks #1 and #3. Engraved,

[45   ]

'Belonging to the C^{hh} of Christ/in Newtown/1740.' ACS, p. 73; OSAC, p. 323. Owner, First Church, Newton, Mass.

245 *Tankard.* H, 8 1/4"; DM, 4"; DB, 5". Mark #4. Engraved in shield, 'The Gift/of/Nath^n Thomas Esqr/to the First/Church of Christ/in/ Plymouth/1745.' OSAC, p. 376. Owner, First Parish, Plymouth, Mass.

246–247 *Tankards.* Pair. H, 6 1/2"; DM, 3 3/4"; DB, 4 1/4". Marks #1 and #3. Engraved, 'The Gift of/Lie^{nt} Jona^n Lawrence/to the Church of/Christ in Groton/Ob^t Sep^{tmbr} 19/1729.' ACS, p. 74; OSAC, p. 191. Owner, First Parish, Groton, Mass.

248 *Tankard.* H, 7 3/4"; DM, 4 1/8"; DB, 5". Mark #2. Engraved, 'The Gift of/Captn Iohn Brand/Deceas'd to the first/Church.' ACS, p. 72; OSAC, p. 254. Owner, First Church, Lynn, Mass.

249 *Tankard.* H, 7 3/4"; DM, 4 1/8"; DB, 5". Mark #3. Engraved, 'The Gift of Theo: Burrill Esq/to the first Church of Christ in/Lynn'; and above the midband, the Burrill arms. ACS, p. 75; B, p. 26; OSAC, p. 254. Owner, as above.

250 *Tankard.* H, 8". Mark #6. Engraved, 'R/M·A.' Owner, unknown.

251 *Tankard.* H, 8 1/2". Mark #2. Engraved on handle, 'AAT' (for Asa Alfred Tufts), 'JWT' (for John W Tufts), 'TM to AM' (Thaddeus Mason to Anne Mason). Owner, Mrs. Breckenridge Long, Laurel, Md.

252 *Tankard.* H, 7 5/8"; DM, 4"; DB, 4 7/8". Mark #2. Engraved, 'The Gift of/Mrs Susanna Sharp/to the Church in/Brooklin/1770'; on handle, 'S/R S' (for Robert and Susanna Sharp). ACS, p. 71; OSAC, p. 100. Owner, First Parish, Brookline, Mass.

253 *Tankard.* With pineapple finial. H, 9 1/16"; DB, 5 1/4". Marked #5 twice. Engraved, 'C/N E/1770.' (Tulip engraved between N and E. Initials for Nathaniel and Elizabeth Curtis, m. 1738.) Owner, W. M. Jeffords, Pennsylvania.

254 *Tankard.* With mask tip. H, 9 1/8"; DM, 4 3/8"; DB, 5 5/8". Mark #2. Engraved, 'D/T E' (for Timothy and Experience Dwight) and the Dwight arms, with mantling. Owner, Professor Herbert B. Dwight, M.I.T., Boston.

255 *Tankard.* Mask tip and pineapple finial. H, 9 1/4"; DM, 4 1/4"; DB, 5 1/4". Marks, #2 on body, #4 on lid. Scratched on bottom, 'M C.' Engraved, impaled coat of arms (unidentified). Owner, Garvan.

256 *Tankard.* Mask tip. H, 8 3/8"; DM, 4"; DB, 5 1/4". Mark #5. Engraved with festoons, 'The Gift/of/THO WELLS Esq/Decd to the Church of/Christ in/DEAR-FIELD/1750.' OSAC, p. 136. Owner, First Congregational Church, Deerfield, Mass.

257 *Tankard.* Mask tip and hinge decoration. H, 7 3/4"; DM, 4"; DB, 5 7/8". Mark #2. Engraved, on handle, 'B/I ॥ L'; scratched on bottom, '29-19-0.' (Cover skilfully restored.) Owner, George C. Gebelein, Esq., Boston.

Silver Made by Jacob Hurd

258 *Tankard*. Mask tip. H, 8 3/8"; DM, 4"; DB, 5 1/8". Mark #2. Engraved on handle, 'G/E ⫒ A'; scratched on bottom, 'E Grant/28 18 12.' Owner, Herbert Lawton, Esq., Boston.

259 *Tankard*. Mask tip. H, 8 1/2"; DM, 4"; DB, 5 1/2"; Wt, 31 oz. 1 dwt. Engraved with the Saltonstall arms, and on bottom, in recent letters, 'L.S.1825–1895/R.M.S. 1859–1922/L.S.1892–.' AS, p. 69. Owner, Hon. Leverett Saltonstall, Chestnut Hill, Mass.

260 *Tankard*. Decorated tip. H, 8 1/2". Marks, #2 on body, #4 on lid. Engraved, 'W/S * S' on handle. AS, p. 66. Owner, unknown.

261 *Tankard*. Mask tip with small hammered nose at rim. H to finial tip, 9"; DM, 4"; DB, 5 1/2". Engraved with decorative monogram of William Lithgow and date, '1751.' Owner, Mrs. Paul M. Hamlen, Boston.

262 *Tankard*. Flame finial and small hammered nose at rim. H, 8 13/16"; DB, 5 1/16". Marked #2 twice. Engraved with the Whipple arms. Owner, Mrs. Harvey H. Bundy, Boston.

263 *Tankard*. Moulded drop at hinge. H, 7"; DB, 5"; DM, 4 1/8"; Wt, 25 oz. 10 dwt. Marks, #2 on body, #3 on lid. Engraved, 'W/I * M' (for John and Mary Walker of Kittery, m. 1717). Modern inscription giving descent to present owner on front. Owner, Frank A. Walker, Braintree, Mass.

264 *Tankard*. Mark #2. Engraved. 'W/I S' (for Isaac and Sarah Winslow), and the Winslow arms. Owner, Hon. Winslow Warren, Dedham, Mass. (in 1934).

265 *Tankard*. H, 8 1/2"; Wt, 26 1/2 oz. Mark #2. Owner, William T. H. Howe, Esq., Cincinnati, Ohio.

TEAPOTS. With the exception of the four items to be last listed, and which are nearly pear-shaped, all of Jacob Hurd's teapots have a globular body, on a moulded round base, with curved spout, silver sockets curved wooden handle, flush hinged lid, with wood finial and silver tip, and with decorative engraving about cover and on shoulder of body. Any exception to this will be noted in the listing.

266 *Teapot*. H, 6". Marked twice #4. Engraved, The Clapp(?) arms with, in ribbon below, 'EX DONO PUPILLORUM 1745.' A presentation piece to President Clapp of Yale from the students. Owner, George M. Grinnell, Esq., a descendant.

267 *Teapot*. H, 5 1/4"; W, 15" (including handle), 7" (body). Mark #2. Engraved, the Pepperell arms and on bottom, 'R B.' AS, p. 67. Owner, Garvan.

268 *Teapot*. Spout with octagonal shape next body, with raised band. H,

[47]

5 1/2''; W, 9 1/4''. Mark #3. Engraved, the Townsend arms, with 'The Gift of Jam^s Townsend/to Reb. Mason/1738.' Owner, Garvan.

269 *Teapot*. Spout with band and panels. H, 5 5/8''; D, 4 1/2''. Mark #3. Engraved, the Bradford arms. Owner, Institute of Arts, Detroit, Mich.

270 *Teapot*. Like above. H, 5 1/8''; DB, 3 3/8''; Wt, 15 oz. 4 dwt. Mark #3. Engraved, the Flynt arms, and 'Ex dono Pupillorum/1738.' HTC, p. 141. Owner, Edward J. Holmes, Esq., Boston. (Gift to Henry Flynt, Harvard Tutor, 1699–1754.)

271 *Teapot*. Like above. H, 5 1/2''; D, 4 3/4''; Wt, 13 oz. 11 dwt. Mark #2. Engraved, the Andrews arms, and a double cipher, 'M S' (?); on bottom, 'S/S M'/(note the second 'S' was originally 'E'). ASC, p. 72. Owner, MFA, Boston.

272 *Teapot*. Like above. H, 6 1/2''; D, 4 1/2''; DB, 3 3/8''; W, 9''; Wt, 17 oz. 5 dwt. 12 gr. Mark #3. Engraved, the Holyoke arms. HTC, p. 37. Owned by private collector.

273 *Teapot*. Like above, but with silver pineapple finial above wood knob. H, 5 3/4''; D, 5''; DB, 3 5/16''; Wt, 17 oz. 15 dwt. Mark #2. Engraved, 'M Perit/Maria Perit Gilman,' and on bottom, 'G/D ‖ R.' Owner, Henry F. du Pont, Esq., Delaware.

274 *Teapot*. Like above with pineapple finial, but with silver handle, ivory insulated. H, 5 3/4''; D, 5''. Mark #4. Engraved with the Whipple arms. Owner, Museum of Art, Cleveland, Ohio. (See their Bulletin #7.)

275 *Teapot*. With panelled spout, silver pineapple finial and repoussé work on shoulder. H, 5''; D, 4 5/8''; DB, 3 5/16''; H (total), 6 1/2''. Mark #4. Engraved, the Fleet arms. Owner, MFA, Boston.

276 *Teapot*. Small panelled, slightly curved, spout, flat loose cover, bayonet joint and turned silver finial above wood knob. H, 4 1/16'', total 5 1/8''; DB, 3''; L, 8 1/8''. Marked twice #3. Engraved, the Gibbs arms, and on bottom, '1735' in old figures, with, in late lettering, 'Lydia from Grandmother Prescott 1812/Dorothy from her Great Aunt Lydia 1891.' B, p. 66. Owner, Miss Dorothy Miner, Brookline, Mass.

277 *Teapot*. H, 6 5/8''; D, 5 1/8''; Wt, 18 oz. Engraved, the Coffin arms. (In South Kensington Museum, London.) Owner, Victor A. Watson, Esq., London, Eng.

278 *Teapot*. H, total, 6 1/2''. Mark #6. Engraved on socket, 'T/C + S' (for C. and S. Tilden). Owner, Mrs. J. E. Muggah, Glace Bay, Cape Breton, Nova Scotia.

279 *Teapot*. H, total, 5''; D, 4''. Mark #1 on bottom, #3 on lid. Engraved on bottom, 'E Storer 1756/W S E 1874' (Eaton) and the Sturgis arms on side. ACS, p. 74. Owner, MFA, Boston.

280 *Teapot*. H, 4 3/4''. Mark #1. Owner, Miss Caroline Parsons.

281 *Teapot*. H, total, 6''; D, 4 3/4''. Mark #3. Engraved, the Henchman

PLATE XI

Silver Made by Jacob Hurd

arms with Burrill crest and 'The Gift of Theo: Burrell Esqr/to the Rev^d Mr Nath Henchman/Pastor of ye first Church in Lynn/July 5th 1737.' Owner, Philip L. Spalding Estate, Boston.

282 *Teapot.* H, total, 5 1/2", to lid, 4 1/16"; D, 4 5/8"; L, 8 7/8". Mark # 6. Engraved on bottom, 'W/I A' and arms of Symmes impaling Wolcott. Wts, scratched on bottom, '14–10–0 & 13–4.' Owner, George S. Parker, Esq., Salem, Mass., whose family acquired it in 1785.

283 *Teapot.* Slightly pear-shaped body with straight spout. H, 5 3/4"; W, 6 1/8". Marked # 2 twice. Engraved on side, 'W McK'; on bottom, 'G/F R.' Owner, Mrs. Breckenridge Long, Laurel, Md.

284 *Teapot.* Nearly pear-shaped body, with pineapple finial. H, 5 3/4"; D, 4 3/4"; DB, 3 1/4"; W, 10 1/2". Mark # 4. Engraved, 'C/M ‖ W' on bottom. (This piece originally had a coat of arms, and an inscription on sides, which were cut out and new silver sides restored.) Owner, George C. Gebelein, Esq., Boston.

285 *Teapot.* Nearly pear-shaped body. H, 6"; W, 8". Mark # 2. Engraved, with a nearly obliterated inscription. Owned by a private collector.

286 *Teapot.* Pear-shaped body. H, 6"; D, 4 1/4"; DB, 3 3/8"; W, 9 1/2". Mark # 5. Engraved, the Sherburne arms. Owner, Erving Pruyn, Albany, N.Y.

287 *Thimble.* Gold, usual shape, with indented top, and quaint leafy scrolls on body above moulding. H, 5/8"; D, 5/8". Mark # 3. Engraved, 'Eliz^h Gooch,' in early letters, with '1714' added later. (Hurd could not have made thimble in 1714, but probably in 1727 when Eliz^h Gooch was born.) Owner, Garvan.

288 *Tray.* Octagonal body, with piecrust rim, indented corners, curved legs, and paw feet. D, 13 1/4"; H, 1 5/8". Mark # 4. Engraved with scroll decoration on face, with 'A M/to/S M' in large script in centre. Owner, Mrs. O. L. Clark, Amherst, Mass.

289 *Tray.* Circular piecrust body on three cut scroll feet, with engraved border inside rim. D, 11 3/4"; H, 2"; Wt, 27 oz. 12 dwt. Mark # 4. Fine shield in centre, handsome scrolls surrounding, but arms and crest erased. ACS, p. 77. Owners, the Misses Townsend, Boston.

290–291 *Trays.* Pair of small salvers, octagonal form, with moulded rims on four bandy legs with hoofed feet. D, 6 1/4". Mark # 4. Engraved, the Hastings arms, and on bottom, 'H/A T/1750.' ACS, p. 126; B, p. 77. Owner, Hollis French, Esq., Boston.

292 *Tray.* Octagonal body, with indented corners, on four small club feet. Inner edge of rim decorated with engraved ropes, tassel at corners. D, 7". Mark # 2. Engraved with unidentified arms in centre. Owner, Henry F. du Pont, Esq., Delaware.

293 *Tray.* Square salver, with gadrooned rim, on four feet. D, 9". Mark # 2. Engraved, the Browne arms. B, p. 24. Owned by private collector.

[49]

Silver Made by Jacob Hurd

294 *Tray.* Engraved, 'R/G E.' Owner, in 1927, Mrs. Carl G. Betton, Boston.

295 *Tray.* D, 6″. Mark #6. Engraved, 'J. Q. 1742.' Owner, Edmund Quincy, Esq., Boston.

296 *Tray.* Large salver, octagonal shape, with piecrust rim, on four scroll feet, with decorative border engraved inside rim. L, 12 15/16″; W, 12 11/16″; Wt, 34 oz. 1 dwt. 15 g. Mark #4. Engraved, the Clarke arms in a shell and acanthus cartouche. Owner, Garvan.

Silver Made by Nathaniel Hurd

297 *Basket.* Body a half-keg form with three hoops and bail handle. H, 3 3/8"; D, 2 5/8". Mark # 9. Engraved, 'R : S' (for Rebecca Salisbury, 1731–1811), and 'M' (later) for Mason. Owner, Worcester Art Museum.

298–299 *Beakers.* Pair with bell-shaped bodies on high moulded circular bases. H, 6 1/2"; DM, 4 1/2"; DB, 3 3/8". Mark # 9. Engraved, the Hancock arms, crest a demi-griffin; and below, 'The Gift of the Honorable/ Thomas Hancock Esq/to the Church of Christ in Lexington/1764.' OSAC, p. 246. Owner, First Congregational Society, Lexington, Mass.

300 *Can.* Engraved with the Lloyd arms, at South Kensington Museum, London. Owner, Victor A. Watson, Esq., London, Eng.

301 *Can.* Standard shape, with round flanged base, double scroll handle with acanthus leaf. H, 5". Mark # 9. Engraved, unknown coat of arms. Owner, Mrs. J. E. Marble, South Pasadena, Cal.

302 *Coffee Pot.* Can or pear-shaped body, on round moulded base, with domed cover and flame finial, swan's-neck spout with body drop, silver sockets, and ebony handle. H, 9 1/4". Mark # 10. Engraved with Chauncy and Stoddard arms impaled. (Rev. Charles Chauncy m. Mary Stoddard in 1765.) Owner, Mrs. A. C. Nason, Newburyport, Mass.

303 *Cream Jug.* Pear-shaped body, everted lip with serrated edge, double scroll handle, on three bandy legs with scalloped feet. H, 3 1/2". Mark # 10. Engraved, the Hickling arms, with Chippendale decoration, and on bottom, 'S. Hickling,' in old script, with 'to S H L' in later script. OSAC, p. 80. Owner, Garvan.

304 *Cream Jug.* Like above. H, 3 3/4". Mark # 11. Engraved, '1766.' OSAC, p. 79. Owner, Ray Baker Taft, Esq., Hingham, Mass.

305 *Loving Cup.* Bell-shaped body, moulded midband, two single scroll acanthus handles, on a high moulded base, with loose moulded cover with round finial. Gadrooning and repoussé decoration. H, 13 1/4"; W, 11 3/4"; DM, 5 5/8"; Wt, 71 oz. 8 dwt. Mark # 9. Engraved, the

Silver Made by Nathaniel Hurd

Whitechurch arms with Maddock's crest (1758). See *Antiques*, September, 1932. Owner, Mrs. Breckenridge Long, Laurel, Md.

306 *Marrow Spoon.* L, 8″. Mark # 10. Owner, Hermann F. Clarke, Esq., Boston.

307 *Sauce Boat.* Deep wide bowl, long everted lip, scalloped rim, double scroll handle, 3 bandy legs with wide hoofs. H, max. 4 1/8″, to rim, 2 1/4″; L, 6 3/4″; Wt, 12 oz. 14 dwt. Mark # 10. Engraved, on bottom 'S * W' (probably Sarah Warren). AS, p. 69. Owner, Richard W. Hale, Esq., Boston.

308 *Seal.* Metal (steel?) in silver mount with ivory handle. D, 1″; L, handle, 3 1/2″. Mark # 10. The Mather arms. Owner, private collector.

309 *Seal.* Circular silver die for embossing. D, 2″. Mark # 9. Design, ship arriving at port with sun breaking through storm clouds. Made for, and still owned by, Boston Marine Society, 1754.

310 *Seal.* Made in 1752 for the Provincial Grand Lodge of Masons in Boston, but misplaced.

311 *Skewer.* Plain tapering shaft, rectangular section, with loop at end. L, 13 1/4″. Mark # 3. Owner, Edward H. R. Revere, Esq., Boston.

312 *Spoon.* Double drop, rib end. L, 8″. Mark # 9. Engraved, crest, out of a ducal crown, a demi-horse. Owner, Mrs. Paul M. Hamlen, Boston.

313 *Spoon.* Single drop, rib front. L, 8 1/4″. Mark # 9. Engraved, 'M/I = M.' Owner, George C. Gebelein, Esq., Boston.

314 *Spoon.* L, 4 1/2″. Mark # 12. Engraved, 'S/D I.' Owner, Mrs. H. F. Clarke, Boston.

315 *Spoon.* Elliptical bowl, single drop and shell. L, 4 1/2″. Mark # 9. OSAC, p. 80. Owner, Dwight Blaney, Esq., Boston.

316–317 *Spoons.* Pair with feather edge. L, 5 1/8″. Mark # 10. Engraved, Hutchinson crest. Owner, Garvan.

318 *Spoon.* Single drop and shell. Feather-edge handle, with back rib. L, 4 1/2″. Mark # 12. Owner, George C. Gebelein, Esq., Boston.

319 *Teapot.* Pear-shaped body, curved spout with moulding and drop, silver sockets with curved wood handle. Round moulded base, domed lid, flame finial, flush joint and hinge. Fine engraved decoration on lid, about opening and at upper socket. H, max. 6 1/2″; H, body, 5″; D, 4 3/4″; DB, 3 3/8″. Mark # 10 twice. Engraved, the Stoddard arms. Owner, Miss Margaret Hall, North Cohasset, Mass.

320 *Teapot.* Similar to above, but with spiral finial. H, 5 3/4″. Mark # 10. Engraved, the Gibbs arms. Owner, Hollis French, Esq., Boston.

321 *Teapot.* Globular body, curved spout, silver handle with ivory insulators, flush-hinged domed lid with acorn finial, moulded round base. Scrolls and mask decoration surrounding lid. H, 5 7/8″. Mark # 9. Engraved, the Howard coat of arms, and on the other side, '1776.' OSAC, p. 80. Owner, Mrs. Francis Woodbridge, Falmouth, Me.

PLATE XII

Silver Made by Benjamin Hurd

322 *Baptismal Basin.* Circular body, deep well, flat rim and no boss. D, total, 11 3/4"; D, well, 8 1/4". Rim, 1 3/4"; Dpth, well, 3". Mark #14. Engraved on rim, 'The Gift of Francis/White Esq to the First/Protestant Dissenting/Church in Halifax/October 25ᵗʰ 1769.' Owner, Saint Matthew's United Church, Halifax, N.S.

323 *Baptismal Basin.* Circular body, deep well, with domed boss and flat rim. D, 11 3/8"; Dpth, 2 7/8". Mark #13. Engraved on rim, 'The Gift of/Mr John Mory/To the Second Church of Christ in/Roxbury/1774.' OSAC, p. 491. Owner, Second Church of West Roxbury, Mass.

324 *Cream Jug.* Pear-shaped body, serrated rim, long spout, double scroll handle, three duck feet with three lobes. H, 4"; D, 2 1/4". Marked #13 twice. Engraved, on front in cipher, about 1860, 'C J Y' (for Caroline J. Young). Owner, Robert H. Stevenson, Esq., Boston.

325-328 *Spoons.* Four, with double drop and rib front. L, 8". Mark #15. Engraved, 'S * Z.' Owners, Garvan Collection, Hollis French, Esq., Boston, and P. Hammerslough, Esq., Hartford, Conn.

329 *Spoon.* L, 8". Mark #13. Engraved, 'S H.' Owner, Henry G. Lord, Esq., New York.

330 *Spoon.* Single drop, decorated shell, rib front. L, 8". Mark #13. Engraved, 'A ·:· W.' Owner, George C. Gebelein, Esq., Boston.

331-335 *Spoons.* Five, single drop, decorated shell, bent handle, feather edge, rib on back. L, 4 3/8". Mark #13. Engraved, 'R ·:· A.' Owners, one by Hollis French, Esq., four by George C. Gebelein, Esq., Boston.

336 *Spoon.* Like above. L, 4 7/8". Mark #13. Engraved, 'P ·:· G.' Owner, Mrs. E. P. Hamilton, Milton, Mass.

Nathaniel Hurd

GOLDSMITH AND ENGRAVER

1730–1778

Nathaniel Hurd
Goldsmith and Engraver

NATHANIEL was the fourth child of Jacob Hurd and his wife Elizabeth. He was born in Boston the 13th of February, 1729, Old Style, or the 24th of February, 1730, according to our present calendar.

His parents moved to Roxbury not long after his birth. He attended the Boston Latin School, entering in 1738 at the age of nine. No doubt he was apprenticed to his father, or at least brought up to learn his trade in Jacob's shop, and early showed talent for silversmithing, engraving, and die-cutting. On coming of age a few years before his father's death, we find him located in Boston. He never married.

Two years after his father died, he advertised in the *Boston Gazette* of April 28, 1760, as follows:

> Nathaniel Hurd informs his customers he has remov'd his shop from MacCarty's corner,[1] on the Exchange, to the back part of the opposite Brick Building where Mr. Ezekiel Price Kept his Office. Where he continues to do all sorts of Goldsmith's Work. Likewise engraves in Gold, Silver, Copper, Brass and Steel, in the neatest Manner, and at reasonable Rates.

[1] The westerly corner of what is now State and Congress Streets.

Nathaniel Hurd, Goldsmith and Engraver

From this it would appear that the association between the two Hurds, Nathaniel and Benjamin, together with their brother-in-law, Daniel Henchman, who were with Jacob before his death, had been severed, and probably the three former apprentices now had separate shops.

Mr. Ezekiel Price, mentioned in the advertisement, was a well-known notary, and confidential secretary to several royal governors. For him Nathaniel designed a handsome bookplate which will be described elsewhere herein.

Nathaniel must have been learning engraving and silver-smithing early, for he certainly engraved some of his book-plates before the age of twenty. His first dated one is 1749, but a number show cruder work and were undoubtedly en-graved before that time.

His first silver was presumably made in his father's shop and probably bore Jacob's mark. It was not until 1764 that we find a dated piece of his silver, but many must have been made before that year. He probably began marking his own pieces by 1758 and possibly by the time he was of age in 1751.

It was in 1754 that he engraved the trade card for J. Palmer, the tallow chandler, which is the earliest dated piece of his engraving, as distinguished from his bookplates, though some of his undated ones must have been earlier.

On March 12, 1759, and for the next two years in succession, Nathaniel was 'chose' one of the clerks of the market, and later, in 1760 and 1761, he was selected as scavenger, there being one for each ward, his ward being No. 9.

In the books of the Record Commissioners [1] we find entries showing that in 1759 Nathaniel was sworn in as 'Fire Ward.' It was the duty of the watch to see that the great hogsheads, standing in certain places in the town, were kept full of water, and that the street lights on selected houses were lighted by

[1] See *Record Commissioners*, vol. 16, pp. 18, 34, 49, 236, and 270.

[58   ]

the owners so that they would be available in case of fire. In this event, the fire wards, whose wand of office was a staff five or six feet long, colored red, and headed with a bright brass spire six inches long, had all necessary authority in the putting out of fires.

Again, in 1760, Nathaniel was chosen to examine the accounts of Boston lotteries, Numbers 7, 8, and 9, by which the town raised money for various objects.

These public offices seem to be all that he filled, except that in 1770 he was one of the jury at the inquest of a victim of the Boston Massacre, Michael Johnson by name, alias Crispus Attucks. Their finding was

> That the said Michael Johnson was wilfully and feloniously murdered at King street in Boston in the County aforesaid on the Evening of the 5th instant between the hours of nine and ten by the discharge of a Musket or Muskets loaded with Bulletts two of which were shot thro' his body by a party of Soldiers to us unknown then & there headed and commanded by Captain Thomas Preston of his Majesty's 29th Regiment of foot against the peace of our Sovereign Lord the King his Crown & dignity and so by that means he came by his death as appears by evidence.

Regarding Nathaniel's private life there is little recorded, less even than we have learned of his public activities; but there is one fact which shines out from his will and that is that he had a great affection for his brothers and sisters and their families.

This document shows that he was generous, for he cancelled all debts that his brothers owed him, indicating in the first place that he was successful in business and had money to leave, and secondly, that he was glad to give it to those who needed it. He was much interested in his nephews, and to his namesake, Nathaniel Hurd Furnass, he bequeathed £30, and to the latter's brother John [1] he left his large printing-press and some tools 'in consideration of the Love I bear to him and the Genius he discovers for the same business which I have followed & to which I intended to have brought him up to.'

Excepting his small silver watch marked 'Brown Boston on the Face of it,' [2] which he left to his printer, Thomas Fleet, and £15, which he bequeathed to Polly Sweetser who nursed him in his last sickness, everything was left to his family, Benjamin in particular being a considerable beneficiary.

The fact that he owned a number of prints indicates a taste for art which one might expect in a man of his nature. His short will which follows is worth perusing, as it gives one an insight into his last days. His will was signed the 8th of December, 1777. What it was that carried him off we do not know, but he must have been ill for some time, or he would not have left a bequest to Miss Sweetser for nursing, nor would his signature have been as illegible as it appears on the will signed on his deathbed, as compared with his usual bold autograph on other papers; for example, on the Fayerweather Receipt, both of which are shown on page 62.

NATHANIEL'S WILL

Whereas I Nathaniel Hurd of Boston in the County of Suffolk & State of Massachusetts Bay Goldsmith & Engraver being Sick & weak in Body but of Perfect mind & memory Do therefore make and ordain this my last Will & Testament as touching

[1] John Mason Furnass, engraver and portrait painter, was the son of John Furnass and Anne Hurd Furnass, sister of Nathaniel Hurd, the engraver. Furnass was painting portraits in Boston in 1785. He was born November 11, 1762, and died of epilepsy at Dedham, Massachusetts, June 22, 1804. He made at least two portraits of John Vinal, the old schoolmaster of Boston. (Dunlap's *History of the Arts of Design in the United States*, vol. III.)

[2] Probably made by Gawen Brown, the well-known clockmaker of Boston, b. 1719, d. 1801.

PLATE XIII

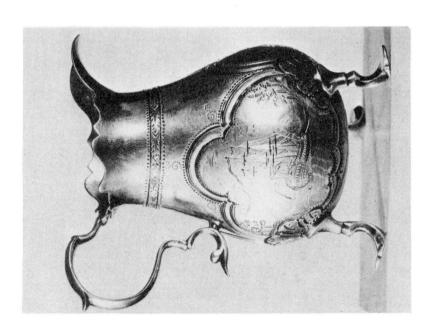

Nathaniel Hurd, Goldsmith and Engraver

such Wordly Estate wherewith it hath pleased God to bless Me in this Life —— And first I give & Bequeath to my Brother Jacob Hurd now of Halifax the Sum of Twenty Pounds for Silver Spoons, or other piece of Plate he may chuse & all that He is indebted to Me ——

To my Brother John Hurd I give & bequeath the like Sum of Twenty Pounds for the like purpose together with My Prints of Richard the 3d & the March to Finchley Common both done by Hogarth & such other Prints he may chuse, and all that He is Indebted to Me ——

To my Brother Benjamin Hurd I give & Bequeath Thirty Pounds, in Tools, Cloaths and some Money, together with the Debt He now owes to Me ——

To my Sister Eliz* Henchman I give & bequeath the Sum of Sixty Pounds in Furniture & Money as She chuses, together with my Minature Picture.

To My Sister Ann Furnass I give & bequeath the Sum of Thirty Pounds in Furniture & Money as She chuses — & to her Son Nat Hurd the sum of Thirteen Pounds as a Legacy for bearing my Name.

And to my Brotherin Law John Furnass the Tobacco Box which has my Name on it, and my Volumes of the Universal Dictionary of Arts & Sciences ——

To my Sisters Walley & Hall I give and Bequeath to each of Them the Sum of Twenty Pounds for Spoons or any thing else they may chuse.

To Thomas Fleet of Boston Printer I give my small Silver Watch (Brown Boston, on the Face of it) in token of the Regard & Friendship which I have for Him ——

To Miss Polly Sweetser I give & bequeath the Sum of Fifteen Pounds for her Kindness and Tenderness to Me in my Sickness & for the Esteem I have for her; and my Bible ruled with Red Lines ——

To my Sister Ann Furnass; oldest Son John Mason I give & bequeath my large Printing Press & some Tools in consideration for the Love I bear to him & the Genius he discovers for the same Business which I have followed & to which I intended to have brought him up to ——

Nathaniel Hurd, Goldsmith and Engraver

The Remainder of Real & Personal Estate which I die possessed of, after my Just Debts, Legacies, Charges &c are paid, I give & Bequeath to my Brother Benj. Hurd & to My Sisters Elizabeth Henchman & Ann Furnass to be divided equally among them & Secured to such of Them as require it in such manner As not to be taken away from them by any of Their Creditors — And I Do will & ordain my Brother in Law John Furnass to be Executor, & my Sister Elizabeth Henchman to be Executrix to this my last Will & Testament;, & I do hereby revoke and Disannul all former Wills, Legacies & Bequeaths, & Confirm this to be my last Will & Testament ——

In Witness whereof I have set my Hand & Seal this Eighth day of December & in the Year of our Lord 1777 ——

(Signed) Nat. Hurd

Signed Sealed & declared
to be his last Will and
Testament in Presence
of Us ——
    Thomas Fleet   *Sw*
    Zech. Brigden   *Sw*
    David Townsend *Sw*

Signature on Receipt   Signature on Will

Nathaniel Hurd, Goldsmith and Engraver

In the Granary Burying Ground there can be found the following inscription which also appears in Bridgman's *Pilgrims of Boston* (Ed. 1856, p. 320):

In Memory of

Mr. Nathaniel Hurd

of Boston

an Eminent Goldsmith & Engraver

who departed this life 17th Dec'r 1777 ae 48 yrs

There are a few scraps of Nathaniel's writing and advertisements which may be of slight interest as throwing side-lights on his daily life, and these are, so far as known:

1. A receipt in writing, dated Boston, July 26, 1765.
   Received of William Palfrey one Pound 16/ in full for a Gold Medal.
   £1.16   Nat. Hurd

2. *Boston Evening Post*, December 27, 1762. Advertisement:
   Engraved and sold by Nath Hurd, a striking likeness of his Majesty King George the Third, Mr. Pitt and General Wolfe fit for a picture or for Gentlemen and Ladies to put in their watches.

3. Advertisement in *Boston Gazette*, November 11, 1765:
   After describing the caricature Liberty Tree print, and the deplorable State of America by Wilkinson, it ends, 'The above to be sold by Nathaniel Hurd, near the Town House.'

4. Advertisement in *Boston News-Letter*, July 17, 1766:
   Prints of the late Rev. Jonathan Mayhew, D. D., done in Metzotinto by Richard Jennys jun. are sold by Nathaniel Hurd, Engraver, near the Exchange.

5. A receipted bill with error in year, the whole of which is in Nathaniel's handwriting, reading:

Nathaniel Hurd, Goldsmith and Engraver

Tho.ˢ Fayerweather Esq.ʳ to Nat. Hurd D.ʳ.

	To taking out Crest's from Salts & putting New	£1 . . 4 —
Boston	To mend.ᵍ Sauce pan & can	12 —
June 16	To Large Crest on Sauce pan	12 —
773	To taking out Arms from Coffee pott & yʳ Arms on D.ᵒ	2 . . 5
	O Tenor	£4 . . 13 —

Rec.ᵈ the Above in full
Nath'' Hurd

It will be noted that this bill is made out in Old Tenor or paper money, concerning which a brief explanation will be found in the sketch of Jacob's life herein. The value of this bill in Massachusetts money of six shillings to the dollar would be $2.07.

    6. Registry of Deeds, vol. 94, p. 231:
        On July 6, 1760, Nat Hurd mtges to Thos Waite for
        £160 a messuage with land behind Half Square
        Court and Leverett Lane (now Congress Street)
        Westerly by land of Powell 24 ft.
        Northerly "   "   " McCarthy 57 ft.
        Easterly including the pump 4 ft.
        Northerly again 10½ ft.

This appears to be the property that Nathaniel bequeathed in equal shares to Benjamin and two of his sisters.

NATHANIEL'S SILVER

Regarding his works, consisting of his silver and seals, his engravings and his bookplates, which two latter are described in detail hereafter, we may say that of the silver now extant there have been listed but twenty-four pieces, as follows:

A basket, a pair of beakers, two cans, a coffee pot, two cream jugs, a covered loving cup, a sauce boat, two seals, a marrow spoon, a skewer, seven spoons, and three teapots.

[64   ]

PLATE XIV

Nathaniel Hurd, Goldsmith and Engraver

These show evidence of a mastery of the craft as taught him by his father. The only marked difference between his design and workmanship and that of Jacob, is in the loving cup and the coffee pot and teapots, which are of the form currently popular in his generation.

The last are of the pear-shaped body type, instead of the globular design of Jacob, and the coffee pot is of elongated pear shape instead of conical. Nathaniel's pieces are more graceful, with better engraving, and his single loving cup is quite different from the two made by his father, and is considerably smaller. The raised decoration on Nathaniel's covered cup, now owned by Mrs. Breckenridge Long, is thought by some to have been added after it left Nathaniel's hands, when it went to England as a gift for Frances, daughter of John White-church, on the occasion of her marriage to John Maddocks in 1758, the year of Jacob's death. This piece remained in England until 1890, when it was discovered and brought back to this country by an enterprising dealer. The puzzling thing about this beautiful piece is the repoussé decoration which will be seen in the illustration and which was not customary on American pieces made by the Hurds. It may have been added in England, though without any English silversmith marks, the only ones being those of Nathaniel Hurd on both body and cover, the latter mark being practically effaced. Were it not for the fact that in raising the decoration on the cover the mark of Nathaniel was erased, it might be that this repoussé was done in his shop, but in that event he would probably have added another of his marks on the lid.

Nathaniel was an ingenious and original craftsman, and can easily be imagined to have been quite capable of this decoration, should his customer have desired it. A detail in connection with the cup is the rather remarkable wooden shipping case, which was evidently made for the cup before it left for

Nathaniel Hurd, Goldsmith and Engraver

England, and in which it was returned to this country. It cannot safely be said that Nathaniel might not have completed the cup as it stands today.

An interesting unsigned description and discussion of this remarkable piece may be found in *Antiques*, vol. XXII, for September, 1932.

As for the other silver made by Nathaniel, it bears evidence of careful and even meticulous design and workmanship, which would be expected from a skilled craftsman and a son and apprentice of Jacob.

The catalogue of his silver, so far as discovered, will be found herein, with that of Jacob, pages 51–52, and his marks, few in number, are as follows:

9. N·Hurd   Initial and surname, pellet between, capitals and lower case in rectangle.

10. N·Hurd   Initial and surname, pellet between, italic capitals and lower case in cartouche with straight lower edge.

11. N·Hurd   Initial and surname, pellet between, Roman capitals and lower case in conforming rectangle.

12. N·H   Initials, pellet between, Roman capitals in rectangle.

Nathaniel Hurd's Seals and Dies

WHILE Nathaniel is said to have engraved seals, the only two examples which the author has found are the one of the Boston Marine Society and a remarkably fine one with the Mather coat of arms on it.

This latter seal, which appears to be cut in steel, is mounted in silver with a turned ivory handle about three inches long. The maker's mark on the silver ferrule is the one with small italic letters in a cartouche with flat bottom, No. 10 on our list of marks. The cutting of the die is unusually precise and delicate and every detail is clear and sharp. The seal is in an ellipse one inch long and seven-eighths inch diameter. The escutcheon itself is one inch long and is perfectly ovoid, but the decoration is slightly Chippendale with scrolls on the sides, two horns rising from the upper part of the shield to frame the crest. The description is as follows:

> Arms: Ermine on a fess wavy azure, three lions rampant.
> Crest: On a torse a lion sejant on a tree-trunk, raguly.
> Motto: None.

The tints on the seal are not indicated in the case of the lions in the fess or crest, but on other Mather arms the lions are shown as of gold and the tree-trunk as green.

[67   ]

Nathaniel Hurd's Seals and Dies

This particular seal was cut by Hurd for the Reverend Moses Mather, first pastor of the Congregational Church in Darien, Connecticut, who was born in 1719 and died in 1806. Moses was a great-grandson of Timothy Mather, who was a brother of Increase and an uncle of Cotton.

The right of this American family to bear these arms is not absolutely clear. Whitmore (*Heraldic Journal*, VI, pp. 21, 22) says that the coat appears in the 'Promptuarium Armorum' under the name of Mather, and this might be thought to be convincing, but it is quite possible that this very manuscript is the source from which the American family took the arms that they used. Papworth gives the arms as those of Madder or Modder of Staffordshire, whereas the Mathers came from Lancashire. Proof of the use of arms by a member of the family earlier than one of the fourth generation here would be desirable evidence in the case.

Cotton Mather's son says in the biography of his father that it is not a 'matter of much consequence that in our coat of arms we bear [1] Ermine, on a Fess wavy azure, three lions rampant or; for a Crest, on a wreath of our colours, a Lion Sedant or on a trunk of a Tree vert.'

While the Reverend Samuel minimizes the fact that his family is armigerous, it is evident that he is proud of it, which is certainly excusable.

Another seal appears on the will of Increase Mather in Suffolk Registry of Deeds, but it is not particularly heraldic, and was evidently drawn to use the flower of the madder, which was an early name for Mather. The device has little interest or significance, except that, if Increase designed it for his own use, for certainly Hurd did not, it might appear that either he did not know or did not care for the right to bear the arms that his grandson mentions. In this connection the remarks on

[1] Description corrected of obvious errors.

[68   ]

PLATE XV

Nathaniel Hurd's Seals and Dies

pages 57–60 of Kenneth Murdock's *Portraits of Increase Mather* are of interest.

The other seal of Nathaniel's is that of the Boston Marine Society, concerning which two entries from their records, sent by courtesy of their Secretary, Captain Joseph I. Kemp, seem to cover the subject completely.

> 5th February 1754
>
> Isaac Freeman, Jere Gridley esq. Jona. Smelling, Giles Tidmarsh, Lewis Turner, were appointed a committee to Devise a seal for the Society and make report to ye Society ye next Tuesday Ensuing.
>
> February 26, 1754, the Committee made report as follows: 'That the silver seal cut by Mr. Nathaniel Hurd, and now presented to the Society by the Committee appointed for that purpose representing a Ship arriving at the light House from a storm and the Sun breaking out of the clouds with the inscription Marine Society at Boston in New England A D 1754 be the Seal of this Society.' So Voted.

This very seal is in use by the Society today.

The Masonic Seal. In looking through the Museum of the Masonic Temple at Boston, Mr. John M. Phillips was shown a wrapping paper which was endorsed 'Seal by Nathaniel Hurd

1752.' It therefore appears that a seal had been made for the fraternity by Nathaniel, though at present it cannot be located.

The Wilmott Seal. In the collection of the Massachusetts Historical Society there is a receipt in Nathaniel's handwriting reading as follows:

> The Honble Thomas Hancock Esqr to Nat Hurd Dr
> To Engraving one Large Seal for Governor   L M°
> Wilmott, with his Coat of Arms   £7 ˙˙ 0·0
> Boston Sept 17, 1763
>   Rec^d the Above in full
>   Nath˙ Hurd

Montague Wilmott was a British Army officer who went to Nova Scotia in 1754, and was Governor of that Province, from 1764 to 1766, dying May 20, 1766. No doubt he was in friendly or business relations with Thomas Hancock, uncle of John, and probably ordered his seal through him. The initials 'L M" probably mean 'Lawful Money.'

Dies. It is known that Nathaniel was an excellent die-cutter, though but few of his embossing dies have left a record. An interesting example of his work in this field is, however, seen in the series of stamps probably cut by him in 1755 for use in embossing legal documents, in conformity with the Act passed that year by the General Court of Massachusetts.

The dies were: for four pence, a schooner; three pence, a pine tree; two pence, a codfish; while for newspapers, a red-ink stamp for one halfpenny with a bird upon it was used.

The two previous paragraphs were quoted almost verbatim from an unpublished paper of George F. Dow, who was a very accurate antiquarian who must have had some proof of the statement that Nathaniel sunk the dies that were used for the stamps of 1755. Unfortunately, we have not been able to check the facts but as it seems most probable we have included the statement here.

Nathaniel Hurd's Engravings

OF THE fifteen known examples of Nathaniel Hurd's engravings, other than his bookplates, there are none of any great artistic merit, though some are quite good. They are possibly as good as those done by others of his period, but they show no such sureness of touch as his bookplates, even though they were probably done between 1754 and

[71]

1774, when he should have been in his best form. While perhaps the ornamental border of the Loan Certificate is among the best of this group, most of the others detract from rather than add to Hurd's reputation.

It must be remembered that his 'Seth Hudson' and the 'Courtship and Marriage' are early caricatures and show signs of haste. They were merely put out for the amusement of the moment and were not in any way serious. His George III, Pitt, and Wolfe, however, were on a serious subject, but even so, though there was no haste about engraving the vignettes, only the fact that Hurd was quite young can excuse such a poor production.

All of these plates were probably pot-boilers for Nathaniel, and he cannot have taken a great deal of interest in them or he might have done better, and it is to be regretted that he can be given so little praise for this part of his work.

One cannot help wondering if Hurd had had a disappointment in love which led him to speak so bitterly of marriage as he did in his caricature on that subject. Unfortunately, we know so little of his private life that we can only speculate on this subject.

1. PRICE CARD OF JOSEPH PALMER & Co., Chandlers, Boston and Germantown.

This card, size 5⅛″ × 4¼″, engrossed and signed, in script, 'Nat Hurd Sculp,' was printed for a firm who evidently made spermaceti candles in what is now Quincy, and sold them at their store in Boston.

George F. Dow states, in his article on 'Trade Cards' (*Old Time New England*, No. 84), that this sheet was engraved before 1754. If so, it was earlier than any of Hurd's dated engravings, though not as early as his Dering bookplate of 1749.

The frame of the design on this Palmer sheet is an elaborate Chippendale arrangement of scrolls with a diapered background, a heraldic device enclosing the Palmer arms at the centre of the top, and a mask in the middle of the bottom.

PLATE XVI

The inscription is in English at the top and French at the bottom with three lines each.

In the centre is an oval giving a view of whaling with two small boats among a school of quaintly drawn sperm whales gambolling, with hills in the background.

At the sides of the oval are spaces in which may be filled the price of candles per pound and the number thereof, both in English and French.

This card was reproduced in Dow's article, and at that time it belonged to him, but the original has unfortunately disappeared.

2. MASSACHUSETTS BILL OF EXCHANGE

The plate for this bill is 8 3/16″ × 7 3/8″, rectangular with rounded corners, and well-engraved in old script are thirteen lines. An ornamental border, handsomely engraved, of fruits and flowers is at the left, a decorative heading and an impressive address at the bottom, with the words, 'Massachusetts Bay,' three times in the engraved text, twice in well-decorated letters and once in script, making a fine-looking bill of exchange.

It is signed in script at lower right, 'Nathl Hurd sculp.'

The copy at the Massachusetts Historical Society is dated January 21, 1761.

Copy in American Antiquarian Society.

3. GEORGE III, PITT, AND WOLFE

Three portraits in circles, at top Georgius III Rex above; The Right Honorable William Pitt to the left; and to the right, Major-General James Wolfe, the British hero.

Thirteen lines laudatory to the three men, beginning, 'Behold the Best of Kings,' etc., are below the vignettes.

This is a rather poor line engraving, executed and signed by 'Nathaniel Hurd Sculp 1762,' elaborately decorated and hand-colored. A copy belonging to the American Antiquarian Society is in a contemporary frame and well-tinted. Size, 5 3/4″ × 4 1/2″. Advertised in the *Boston Evening Post* December 27, 1762, and described by Fielding, #739.

4. MASSACHUSETTS LOAN CERTIFICATE

As described by Stauffer in # 1749. Line engraving. Highly ornamented rectangle made up of leaves, fruit, etc. In ornamental script above, 'Province of The Massachusetts Bay.'

Inside the rectangle a form printed in type. Size, 7.1" × 8.3".

Signed in broad border to the left, 'Nath-¹ Hurd — Sculp — 1762.'

Copy in New York Public Library.

5. DOCTOR SETH HUDSON 1762

The best description of the incident of Doctor Hudson is given in the *New England Magazine* of 1832, vol. 3, from which we partly quote:

> In the year 1762, there appeared in Boston, a curious character, who called himself *Doctor Hudson*. He gave out that he was a Dutchman; that he was possessed of a large fortune, and was traveling for his amusement. He was dressed very gaily; tried to push himself into genteel company; and, though rather expensive in his appearance, he showed but little money and displayed no resources. He was well watched. After some time, a fellow was detected in putting off a note purporting to be from the Treasurer of the Province, which proved a counterfeit. His name was *Howe;* he confessed he was a partner in villany with *Doctor Hudson*, and that they had been privately engaged in making up a number of the Province notes, which were in high credit in this and the neighboring Provinces, and sold readily at an advanced price. The Doctor was also taken into custody. They were tried and convicted; Hudson was ordered to the pillory and Howe to the whipping-post. The execution of their sentence was accompanied by a collection of an immense crowd, and immoderate exultation.
>
> Hurd immediately put out a caricature print of the exhibition, which excited much attention. Hudson was represented in the pillory, and at a short distance was Howe, stripping, near the Whipping-post. The Devil is represented flying towards the Doctor, exclaiming, '*This is the man for me.*' In front of the print is the representation of a medallion, on which is a profile of Hudson, dressed in a bag-wig, with a sword under his arm, (as he generally appeared before his detection,) partly drawn from the scabbard, with the words '*Dutch Tuck,*' on the exposed part of the blade. Round the edge is — '*The True Profile of the Notorious Doctor Seth Hudson, 1762.*'

The doctor and other characters are represented as addressing the multitude in speeches said to have been written by the celebrated wit and poet, Joseph Green, and shown by inscriptions issuing from the mouths of the figures.

The engraving shows haste in execution and is not particularly interesting or artistic, but it was merely intended to be a caricature. The size is 3 1/4″ × 8 1/2″, and it is unsigned.

A copy is in the Boston Public Library and also the Worcester Art Museum. It is reproduced in Murrell's *American Graphic Humor* and in *Colonial Society of Massachusetts*, vol. 25, pp. 40–43.

6. THE LIBERTY TREE

The Liberty Tree caricature engraving was executed by Wilkinson of Philadelphia and its only connection with Hurd is that he advertised in Boston papers to sell it. See *Boston Post* of November 4, 1765, and *The Gazette* of November 11, 1765.

A recent spirited description of it will be found in Dow's *Arts and Crafts in New England*, pp. 8 and 37, and a contemporary description in a supplement to the *Boston News-Letter* of November 7, 1765. See also No. 20 in Murrell's *American Graphic Humor*.

7. JONATHAN MAYHEW

About 1766 Richard Jennys made a mezzotint portrait of the Rev. Jonathan Mayhew which was printed and sold by Hurd and the American Antiquarian Society owns a copy from the plate.

The advertisement in the *Boston News-Letter* of July 17, 1766 reads:

> Prints of the late Rev. Jonathan Mayhew D. D. done in Metzotinto by Richard Jennys, jun. are sold by Nathaniel Hurd Engraver, near The Exchange.

The subject of the portrait was born in 1720, graduated from Harvard College in 1744, and was pastor of the West Church, Boston, from 1747 to his death in 1766.

8. HARVARD COMMENCEMENT DANCE INVITATION OF 1767

Mr. Barnard and Mr. Oxnard present their compliments to – – – – – – – – and ask the favor of – – – – – – – – – company at a dance at the Town House on Thursday after Commencement.
              (Place for signature) – – – – – – – – – – – – –
N.B. The admission to be declared at the door.
                                        Signed, N Hurd Scp
Size, 4 1/4″ × 2 1/4″. A.A.S. has a modern restrike copy.
Note: The full names of the hosts are Sir Thomas Bernard and Mr. Edward Oxnard.

Bernard, Sir Thomas (1750–1818)

Born at Lincoln, Eng., 27 April 1750. Son of Sir Francis Bernard and Amelia (Offley) Bernard. Educated at a private school in New Jersey (his father being governor of that province) and at Harvard University, in 1767. Returned to England with his father and was called to the bar in 1780. Married, 1782, Margaret Adair. Acquired a considerable fortune and retired from law, to devote his life to the welfare of the poorer classes. Received degree of M.A., 1801, from Archbishop of Canterbury, and LL.D., 1801, from Edinburgh University. Succeeded to baronetcy in 1810. Married as second wife, 1815, Charlotte Matilda Hulse. Died on July 1, 1818, and is buried under the Foundling Hospital.

Oxnard, Edward (1747–1803)

Son of Thomas and Sarah (Osborne) Oxnard. Born in Boston 30 July, 1747. Harvard College 1767. Engaged in business in Portland with his brother. 11 Oct. 1774 married Mary Fox. Being a Loyalist he went to England in 1775, returning in 1785. Died in Portland 2 July 1803. The His. Gen. Register for 1872 has extracts from the diary he kept in England.

Edward Oxnard was the father of Mary Ann Oxnard, b. 1784, who inherited the fine coffee pot made by Nathaniel and illustrated herein.

9. JOSEPH SEWALL

This is described under # 1476 in Stauffer. It is a line engraving in an oval frame in a rectangle resting on a base containing the name with Sewall's coat-of-arms on the lower part of the oval. The figure is shown facing front nearly half length in his pastor's gown. The inscription on the base is

Ob 27 June 1769   Aetat 81

Joseph Sewall D.D.

Pastor of the Old South Church, Boston

Vita Bene — Acta Efficit Senectutum Jacundam

(Life well lived makes old age pleasant)

Engrav'd and sold by Nat Hurd Boston 1768

Size 6 1/4″ × 4″.

From the arrangement of the inscription and the date it is obvious that after Hurd finished the plate in 1768, Mr. Sewall died and the artist added the first line.

As a piece of engraving, this portrait does not compare very favorably with other contemporary likenesses. The Massachusetts His-

PLATE XVII

torical Society owns the original copper plate and the American Antiquarian Society and the New York Public Library have copies.

Joseph Sewall, clergyman, a son of Samuel Sewall, was born in Boston in 1688, graduated from Harvard in 1707, and was pastor of the Old South Church from 1713 to his death in 1769.

10. BOSTON MASSACRE 1770

In the third volume of the *New England Magazine* of 1832 there is a statement referring to Hurd's engravings which says, 'One is a representation of the memorable Massacre of citizens on the fifth of March 1770.'

No print on this subject has ever been found, and it is most probable that the writer of that article confused it with Revere's well-known print and in error ascribed it to Hurd.

11. MASSACHUSETTS COMMISSION

This blank form must have been used for several years. One is dated 1771 and signed by Governor Hutchinson.

It is a folio broadside with a very ornate initial 'B,' in which letter is concealed the signature 'Nath¹ Hurd Sc.'

There are copies in the Massachusetts Historical Society and American Antiquarian Society.

Stauffer # 1748.

12. PHILIP GODFRID KAST

This trade card, engraved and signed in script Nat Hurd Sculp, was executed about 1774 and depicts a Corinthian column at left with an iron crane supporting a hanging sign with a lion wielding a pestle in a mortar.

Kast was an apothecary and had 'His shop at the Sign of the Lyon & Mortar in Salem,' as stated above the crane on the card. Below this is a list of some of the stock 'lately imported from London.'

The exact wording of the Card, which is quaint, may be of interest and is as follows:

> Turlington's Balsam of Life. Bateman's pectoral Drops. British Oyl. Stoughton's Elixir Salutis. Hooper's female pills. Lockyers D° & the freshest & best of Drugs & Medicines of all kinds where Apothecarys &

Docters in Town & Country may be Supply'd with large or small Quanti-
ties at the Cheapest rate. Where also may be had compleat Setts of
Surgeons Pocket Instruments. Marble Mortars Double flint Bottles from
half ounce to a quart with glass Stoppers. together w.th most Kinds of
grocery ware Dye Stuff &.c

N B Doctors & Traders may be as well Supply'd by Letter as if present
Themselves.

Nat Hurd Sculp

This particular copy is owned by the American Antiquarian Society,
and is 5 3/4″ × 7 3/4″. It is reproduced in *Old Time New England*,
Serial No. 84.

13. COURTSHIP AND MARRIAGE

This is a reversible caricature showing heads of a man and a woman
with two verses at top and two at the bottom. When viewed in one
position the verse reads:

> Courtship   When fond fools together meet
>   each look gives joy, each kiss is sweet.

When inverted:

> Marriage   That form once o'er with angry brow
>   The married pair both peevish grow.

Signed under caricature, 'Engrav'd & sold by Nat. Hurd Boston.'
Copy in American Antiquarian Society. Undated. Size, 9″ ×
7 3/4″.

14. TABLE OF COINS

This table for changing money, giving weights and values, has no
title, but has an amusing and ornamental heading, showing in the
centre under a semi-circular arch a half-length woman's figure holding
in her left hand a pair of scales, and in her right a palm branch, and
exclaiming (in a ribbon from her lips) FIAT JUSTITIA. On the arch
appear the words,

JAM·REDIT·ET·VIRGO·REDEUNT·SATURNIA·REGNA.

To the left of the arch is seated behind a counter, covered with coins,
a money-changer in a mob-cap, welcoming a young man holding a
large cocked hat and a bag of money.

To the right of the arch is a marine scene with a ship in the offing, while on a lot of boxes sits a well-dressed man, and, hat in hand before him, stands a boy pointing to the ship.

The body of the sheet is divided into two main columns, that on the left is subdivided into columns headed 'COINS, Weights, Value and Lawfull Money,' and the right-hand columns are headed, 'Silver Coins, Weights, Value.' Below the latter columns is a table of the value in ounces of gold and silver.

In the lower left-hand corner is the inscription 'ENGRAV'D, Printed & Sold by Nat^l Hurd.'

The size is 6 1/2″ × 4 3/4″ and it is undated.

An original copy is in the A.A.S. Collection.

15. MASONIC SUMMONS

A line vignette blank to be filled in and issued as a call to meetings held at that time in members' houses.

The design consists of six steps with three columns on each side, Doric, Ionic, and Corinthian, representing Strength, Wisdom, and Beauty. Each column is surmounted by a figure, the ones on the left being Faith, Hope, and Charity, and on the right Britannia, a man and a woman with a child.

Above are three busts probably representing, Solomon, King of Israel, Hiram, King of Tyre, and Hiram Abiff, the three legendary Grand Masters of Free Masonry.

On the arch is a motto, 'Incoctum Generoso Pectus Honesto.' (A generous and honest man has an untroubled heart.)

At the base is the coat of arms of the Provincial Grand Lodge of Masons, with crest and supporters and motto, 'Follow Reason.'

Under the arch suspended from ribbons are a pair of keys saltire, a square, and a pair of crossed pens, representing the Treasurer, the Master, and the Secretary.

At the top of the steps leaning against a column is a plumb on the left and at the right a level.

Within the arch there are fourteen lines of engraved text with blanks for filling in the date, name, and place of the meeting.

The particular blank on exhibition at the Masonic Museum was issued in 1764 to 'Brother Oxnard.'

The summons is signed below the steps at the left, 'Brother N. Hurd, Boston, fecit.' No date. Size, 10 3/8″ × 7 3/8″.

16. ENGRAVED COMPASS DIAL

This line engraving was recently found and presented to the Yale Gallery of Fine Arts by one of Yale's graduates:

> The dial, a card five inches in diameter, bears a star of thirty-two rays, marking the thirty-two points of the heavens, with the East emphasized by engraved scrolls, features found only in nautical instruments. The central part of the star is appropriately engraved with a charming vignette one and one-half inches in diameter, depicting a view of the lighthouse in Boston harbor, encircled by this legend: 'East end of the MARKET BOSTON: Made by AND^r NEWELL.' Engraved in script in the southern point of the star occurs the signature 'N. Hurd Sc^t.' The whole stands out in contrast against a background of finely executed cross-hatching. The compass is encased in a glazed frame of richly colored San Domingo mahogany, eleven and one-half inches in length, with removable sights of boxwood.
>
> Concerning Andrew Newell (1749–1798) little is known other than that he was a maker of mathematical instruments. In the first Boston Directory (1789) he is listed as: 'Andrew Newell, instrument maker, 61 State Street'; while in a later edition (1796) he is listed as being on the 'East side of the Market.'

See *Bulletin of the Associates in Fine Arts at Yale University* for June, 1936, from which the above statement was taken and in which the Dial is illustrated.

17. ZIPHON THAYER

This advertising trade card (Fielding No. 741) is a line engraving vignette. To the left on top of a post is a lion couchant, 'Ziphon Thayer' above a mirror and a chair. There are fifteen lines of engraved text and it is signed 'Nat Hurd Sculp.' Size, 7.6″ × 5.6″.

In the Thayer genealogy there is recorded a Zephion Thayer, b. 1741, m. Mary Lambert 1771, d. 1819. This is probably the one, and he was an upholsterer who had a shop at the head of Water Street for many years, though after the Revolution.

A copy is in the Worcester Art Museum.

18. PROVINCIAL CURRENCY

Two authorities have informed the author that they have seen and examined 'Provincial Currency,' which had been signed by Nathl Hurd, whose signature was concealed in the ornamental engraved

PLATE XVIII

Nathaniel Hurd's Engravings

border, much as it is in the 'Loan Certificate,' and that on some later currency which was printed after the plate became worn, the signature had been erased and Revere's substituted.

Unfortunately a careful search has failed to locate any of these pieces.

As an explanation of this matter the following quotation from an unpublished manuscript of George F. Dow is quite convincing:

> On Oct 13, 1777, the General Court passed an Act that the Treasurer issue notes to exchange for all bills of credit ... and he was authorized to obtain a copper plate for the same. The plate ... was that engraved in 1762 by Hurd. His imprint, 'Nath! Hurd-Sculp — 1762,' had been erased, the border cross-hatched, in an inartistic manner, and for the embossed stamp, had been substituted the figure of an 'American,' holding a sword in right hand and in his left a scroll with the word 'Independence.' This was encircled by the motto, 'Ense petit placidam sub libertate guistem.' The whole design was enclosed in a circle formed by a rattlesnake with thirteen rattles. The word 'State' was also substituted for 'Province.'
> Hurd was mortally ill and died at that time.

In the Archives of the State is a receipted bill against the State from Paul Revere junr. for printing 3000 notes for the use of the State, dated Boston May 25, 1778.

Nathaniel Hurd's Bookplates

O F THE various arts and crafts practised by Nathaniel Hurd, his armorial bookplates stand comparison with those of any artist in this country before or since his time.

After he developed his style and passed the early stages of design and execution, he had a wonderfully sure and bold line, which is very individual, but which led to many imitators, some of whom were clever enough to produce designs which are still difficult to distinguish from Hurd's own work. If imitation is the sincerest flattery, then Hurd was the master he is generally credited to be.

There are listed here more than one hundred and ten varieties and states of the bookplates, but of these there is a total of only fifty-five different family arms, forty of which have been signed by the artist and the remainder are most probably by his hand. There exist other bookplates which some think Nathaniel may have engraved, but these have not been listed, as there appears not enough resemblance to warrant their inclusion.

Undoubtedly, other plates, both signed and unsigned, will be discovered, but probably not many. It has not been possible

[82   ]

for the writer to see all of his known plates, though originals or photographs of all but four have been studied by him.

It has been attempted to ascertain something, even if only a line or two, about the owners for whom the plates were designed, but in some cases even this has not been possible. As it is practical to illustrate only a few plates of different styles, a description of the arms in each case is given, so that one may gain an idea of the various coats, but it has been possible to give the derivation of the arms in only a few cases.

Nathaniel Hurd's portrait by Copley, now owned by the Museum in Cleveland, shows him with one arm resting on two books, the larger of which bears the name 'Display of Heraldry, J. Guillim,' the full title of which is 'A Display of Heraldry by John Guillim, Poursuivant at Arms.'

This volume was published in England and went through several editions, but from the size of the copy shown in the portrait Hurd cannot have used any but the 1724 edition, which we consulted with the hope of tracing the origin of some of the arms used in Nathaniel's plates.

Other American sources in existence in Boston also were consulted. These were the 'Promptuarium Armorum,' the 'Chute Pedigree,' the 'Gore Roll of Arms,' and the 'Miner Pedigree,' though we have no proof that Nathaniel used them. These four manuscripts were available in Hurd's day, and it may be that he saw them, though he probably did not consult them frequently, for only one or two of his coats are represented in them, and it is more probable that the owners suggested to him designs not found in Guillim. There were many families who had old seals or painted coats of arms who might have done this and probably did.

No doubt the appropriation of coats and crests was rife in the colonies, since their use would imply social distinction, and one can imagine that, when a family had emerged from the

[83   ]

Nathaniel Hurd's Bookplates

actual laboring class in this country, they wished to accent the fact by heraldic emblems whether owned rightfully or not.

That there were many families properly entitled to use them is proved by the fact that the Official Committee on Heraldry of the New England Historic Genealogical Society has already recognized and published well over two hundred coats of arms of American families who have the right to use them, and will no doubt approve more when applied for with proper proof.

Many of the provincial families in Hurd's time no doubt had the right to bear arms heraldically, but the fact that Hurd engraved armorial bookplates for them does not prove it, and doubtless some of these were appropriated without proof or privilege.

As an illustration of the desire for a coat of arms, Thomas Jefferson, the great democrat, may be mentioned as having instructed his agent in England to find the coat of arms of his family, and failing that to order a worthy one made.

It is significant that of the two hundred and thirty-four coats accepted by the present Heraldic Committee, only five on that Roll have arms engraved by Hurd.

THE HURD BLAZON

In this connection the case of the Hurd family itself is interesting. In the book of that family by Dena Hurd, it is noted that 'In Shropshire, Surrey and in other home counties in England of this line, the annals date back to 1297, and the Hord arms of this ancestor (John Hord or Hurd, great-grandsire of Jacob the silversmith) have the proper emblazonment with variations as other honors were granted.'

> Arms: Az. a lion rampant or on a chief argent a crane proper between two mullets sable.
> Crest: On a garb a raven proper.
> Motto: Bona Boni. (Good things to the good.)

[84]

PLATE XIX

Nathaniel Hurd's Bookplates

Now John Hord, the first immigrant ancestor of Jacob, landed in Boston by or before 1639, because in that year he was admitted a freeman. He was a 'Taylor' by trade and his son became one and his grandson a joiner. They were evidently people in very modest circumstances and of little education; in fact, John did not even sign his will and had to make his mark only three years before his death. To believe that they belonged to an aristocratic family and had a right to a coat of arms, while possible, is to stretch the imagination.

Nevertheless, Jacob, the great-grandson, had raised himself and his children to a position of affluence when thoughts of heraldry probably came to their minds, and we find Nathaniel designing coats for the prominent citizens and copying the English coat for his family and relatives who undoubtedly used it, as witnessed by the Isaac Hurd plate, and the fact that some of the family are still bearing it today.

Something happened about 1780 concerning this matter, and though it is only supposition, it may be that Jacob's children found reason to question their right to the arms they were using and decided, in view of their now important social position, to petition for a separate and authentic coat. Their father had been a well-known goldsmith, which often in their day meant a banker, though we have no idea that Jacob filled that rôle. He had filled many town offices and was a captain in the militia.

Their brother Nathaniel was a fine silversmith and engraver. Benjamin was also a silversmith and John was a colonel and a successful merchant. So we may well imagine why John, who was the prominent member of the family after Nathaniel's death, petitioned the College of Heralds through his friend, Sir Isaac Heard, at that time Clarenceux, King of Arms, for a new coat of arms. Joined with him in this petition was his nephew, William Foster, by his first wife, Elizabeth Foster.

[85]

Nathaniel Hurd's Bookplates

John Hurd had married in 1783 a second wife, Mary Randall Foster, widow of Isaac Foster (1740–82), although no relative of John's first wife.

Nathaniel Hurd had designed an armorial bookplate for Isaac Foster, who apparently had a right to use it, and it may be that William Foster, a successful merchant, who might have been wrongly using the same arms, desired a coat for himself, as did John, and so joined the latter in the petition to the Heralds' College. It is on record that William Foster was residing in London on April 7, 1783, but whether John Hurd was also there is not known. In any event, their petition was granted them in a quaint document of April 7, 1783, a copy of which was recently obtained from the King's Windsor Herald at London and the text of which follows:

TO ALL AND SINGULAR to whom these Presents shall come RALPH BIGLAND ESQUIRE GARTER Principal King of Arms and ISAAC HEARD ESQUIRE CLAREN-CEUX King of Arms of the South East and West Parts of England from the River Trent Southwards send Greeting: WHEREAS the said CLARENCEUX hath represented unto the Most Honorable CHARLES HOWARD ESQUIRE commonly called Earl of Surrey Deputy with the Royal Approbation to his Father the Most Noble CHARLES DUKE OF NORFOLK Earl Marshall and hereditary Marshal of England that in Testimony of the sincere regard he bears to WILLIAM FOSTER of Boston in New England, MERCHANT now resident in London whose Grandfather THOMAS FOSTER was born in the West of England and settled at Boston aforesaid and of the warm Friendship and Affection which have for a great number of years existed between him the said CLAREN-CEUX and JOHN HURD of Boston aforesaid Esquire Uncle (by Marriage) of the said WILLIAM FOSTER he is extremely desirous that some Variations or Distinctions may be granted and assigned to the Arms used by their Families and therefore requested the Favor of his Lordship's Warrant for our devising

Nathaniel Hurd's Bookplates

and granting such Variations or Distinctions to be borne respectively by the Descendants of JACOB HURD deceased Father of the said JOHN HURD and by THOMAS FOSTER Father of the said WILLIAM FOSTER and his Descendants according to the Laws of Arms. AND FORASMUCH as his Lordship did by Warrant under his Hand and Seal bearing date the third day of April instant authorize and direct Us to devise and grant such Variations or Distinctions in the Arms of HURD and FOSTER accordingly. KNOW YE THEREFORE that We the said GARTER and CLARENCEUX in pursuance of the Consent of the said Deputy Earl Marshal and by Virtue of the Letters Patent of our several Offices to each of Us respectively granted under the Great Seal of Great Britain have devised and do by these Presents grant to the said JOHN HURD the Arms following that is to say AZURE NEPTUNE'S TRIDENT ERECT OR ON A CHIEF WAVY OF THE LAST A RAVEN PROPER Crest on a Wreath of the Colours A BAY HORSE'S HEAD CHARGED WITH TWO ESTOILES IN PALE ARGENT And to the said WILLIAM FOSTER, OR THREE BUGLE HORNS SABLE STRINGED GULES ON A CHIEF WAVY VERT A DOVE RISING PROPER IN THE BEAK AN OLIVE BRANCH GOLD Crest on a Wreath of the Colours A BUGLE HORN INVERTED VERT GARNISHED OR THEREON A VIRGINIA NIGHTINGALE RISING PROPER as the same are respectively in the Margins hereof more plainly depicted the Arms of HURD to be borne by him the said JOHN HURD and his Descendants and by those of his father JACOB HURD aforesaid. And the Arms of FOSTER by the said WILLIAM FOSTER and his Descendants with due and proper Differences according to the Laws of Arms without the Let or Interruption of any Person or Persons whatsoever. IN WITNESS whereof We the said GARTER and CLARENCEUX Kings of Arms have to these Presents subscribed our Names and affixed the Seals of our several Offices this seventh day of April in the twenty third Year of the Reign of our Sovereign Lord GEORGE the THIRD by the Grace of GOD King of Great Britain France and Ireland Defender of the Faith etc. and in

[87   ]

the Year of our LORD One thousand seven hundred and eighty three.

Arms granted Jacob Hurd's descendants, 1783

From this document it will be seen that all male descendants of the names Hurd and Foster have the right to bear these newly granted heraldic devices, and even females can use them so long as they still carry the surname of Hurd.

It is very evident that both Colonel Hurd and his nephew were well known in England, but it seems a little strange that after the Revolution two Americans, at least one of whom, Foster, is known to have been a Patriot, and probably the other also, should wish a heraldic grant from England.

However, the times then were probably little different in some respects from our own, when Americans can still obtain coats of arms from the College of Heralds, if there is a good reason, and they pay the fees.

PLATE XX

Nathaniel Hurd's Bookplates

It had been hoped, when this study of the bookplates was begun, that it would be possible to discover, not only the source of Hurd's authority for his armorial bookplates, but also whether the owner really had the right to use the arms. This has proved impossible of fulfilment and really should not have been expected.

There is a certain number, twenty-eight to be exact, for which the origin is found in Guillim, Hurd's reference book, but of those probably few are capable of being shown to appertain to the provincial families of the same name. Certainly the arms of Dering, Dumaresq, Foster, Livingston, Phillips, Tyler, Vassall, Walker, Wentworth, and others, though not all appearing in Guillim, are rightfully borne.

There may be a good many more who would have such heraldic rights if proof could be obtained, but to trace the blood connection between the bearer of a provincial name and those of the same name who bear arms in England is difficult, very laborious, and often impossible. All we can say is that, of the many families in and about New England using arms, probably a large number have no right to them. Certainly if they depended on Hurd for their authority, it is not of great weight, for it is doubtful if he did other than engrave anything desired, as he was hardly equipped for research in genealogy or in heraldry.

This matter of the use of arms and the right thereto can hardly be better expressed than was done by Allen in his work, *American Book Plates*, where he says on page 113:

> A word must be said about the heraldry on Hurd's book-plates. This science, heraldry, was not held in such general esteem among the New Englanders as it was further south, and while many of the governors and men of high standing in the Northern colonies brought armorial seals with them, a great many who used them did so without strict heraldic authority,

Nathaniel Hurd's Bookplates

and when it became the fashion to use coat-of-arms in various ways, the herald painters of those days who had but slight knowledge of heraldry and who were possessed of a copy of Guillim or some other writer on the subject, would find therein the arms of some family bearing the name of their prospective customer, and without further research would proceed to produce the coat as described. Not always were these arms so ordered correctly borne; indeed, there is much uncertainty about the arms used after about 1730 when our native engravers and painters took up the work of producing arms upon orders. Such seals as were brought by the Colonists from England and such as were used by their descendants are undoubtedly correct, but the questionable arms are those which, as mentioned above, were looked up in this country only, by means of such heraldic works as were at hand. The presence of the arms then on some book-plates cannot be relied upon as sufficient and indisputable proof of their owner's right to them.

Allen lists twenty-eight plates signed by Hurd (excluding the Harvard College plates) and fourteen plates attributed to him. Since 1894, when Allen's list was published, many new Hurds have been discovered, so that now we are able to list fifty-five separate family arms of which forty are signed. This does not count the varieties or states, there being as said previously over one hundred of all kinds.

Nathaniel Hurd's style, though distinctive, had many imitators, among whom Revere was one, and a comparison of their plates shows that the latter was very evidently inspired by Hurd, who was six years his senior and undoubtedly his superior in execution of works of this particular kind.

Hurd used the Chippendale style largely for his plates, although he designed a few in the 'Jacobean' manner and fewer still in the 'Ribbon and Wreath' type, which became the style in England in 1730; with only two yet found having the martial background as decoration.

The reader is no doubt aware that the Chippendale style is

distinguished by an unbalanced shape for the shield, whereas the Jacobean outline is symmetrical. The Ribbon and Wreath style is formed, as its name denotes, with a floral wreath about the escutcheon and a ribbon scroll for the motto. The Jonathan Jackson plate is a typical example of this design, whereas those of Campbell and Murray are examples of the martial treatment. The Andrew Tyler plate, designed for the well-known silversmith of Boston, is one of the most elaborate of Hurd's plates and is very well executed. The Jenkins plate is in about the same class, but perhaps the Peter Livingston, for beauty of design and workmanship, is the best of all and challenges comparison with any armorial bookplate, even if not contemporary.

Hurd's favorite treatment of the decoration surrounding the coats of arms can hardly be called mantling, except perhaps in the case of the Jenkins and Tyler plates. Most of the others have a shell at the bottom, from a hole in which emerges a jet of water. At the sides of a rococo frame surrounding the shield appear scrolls with sprays of stems, leaves, and flowers, while floating from around the crest are frequently scrolls, sometimes architectural in form and at other times almost cloudlike, or resembling drapery.

Frequently the plate has a border consisting of parallel lines enclosing a rope moulding, and occasionally, as in the Wilson plate, with shells at the corners and garlands.

Hurd often put in the upper corners bracketed spaces for the number of the book, but quite as often omitted them.

As for the signature, he seemed to have no fixed practice, but appeared to sign as his mood directed. There are at least sixteen different signatures, varying from N H Sc^p in italics through all combinations of Roman, italic, and script letters, varied with N Hurd and Nathaniel Hurd, and with Sc, Sp, Scp, Sct., Sculp, etc.

[91]

Nathaniel Hurd's Bookplates

Only two of his bookplates are dated, namely, the Benjamin Greene, 1757, and the Thomas Dering, 1749. The small Dering crest, to be sure, had the figures 17—, but this was for the owner to date the acquisition of a book rather than to date the plate itself.

Here follows a detailed description of the bookplates arranged alphabetically. Unless otherwise noted all are in the collection of the American Antiquarian Society at Worcester.

ALLEYNE, THOMAS

    Believed to be of Barbados.

    Arms similar to Alleyne of Penn, except that Burke gives the coat as a lion's head. (See *Heraldic Journal*, V, 4, p. 110.)

    Henry Alline, notary of Boston, 1782, used same arms as did the Alleynes from Barbados.

    Arms: Per chev. arg. and erm, in chief two lions' heads erased or., langued gu.

    Crest: Out of a mural crown, a unicorn's head or.

    Motto: None.

    Name: Thomas Alleyne, in script.

    Style: Chippendale.

    Signed: N H in Roman; Sculp in script.

ANDREWS

    The arms of the Andrews family are engraved on an unsigned plate and without the owner's name. This is in the collection of the A.A.S., and as this plate bears evidence in its design and execution that it is by Hurd, it is so considered here.

    Both Burke and Papworth designate the arms to be those of Andrews. The variations in the charges on the chevrons from roses to quatrefoils or in the tinctures and crest are noted.

    On the bookplate the coat is described as follows:

    Arms: Arg. on a chevron engr. gu. between 3 mullets gu., 3 roses arg.

    Crest: A wolf's head erased proper.

    Motto: Nil admirari (Wonder at nothing).

    Name: None.

PLATE XXI

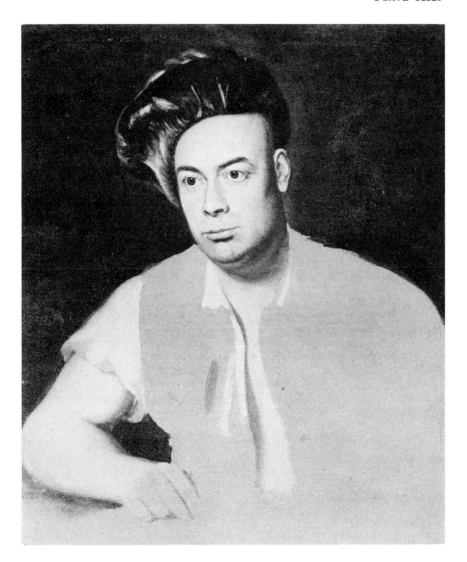

Nathaniel Hurd's Bookplates

Style: Chippendale.

Signed: No signature engraved.

The impression of the plate referred to as owned by the A.A.S. is unfinished in that it has no owner's name engraved thereon, nor number space, nor has it an engraved border which Hurd often used; but on the lower margin is written by pen in fairly old writing the signature D. H. Storer. Now David Humphreys Storer was a Boston physician and a great booklover who was born in 1804 and died in 1891. He was a member of the well-known family who have apparently been using this coat of arms since at least 1723, for in that year Ebenezer Storer married Mary Edwards and on their teapot made by Jacob Hurd, now in the Museum of Fine Arts, the same arms appear with their initials S/EM, though it is to be noted that the letter E has later been changed to S, the reason for which is not evident.

The arms also are displayed on a piece by Thomas Edwards and another by Brigden owned by the Storers originally, and on several other pieces belonging at some time to the family.

In attempting to explain the error in the use of the Andrews arms by the Storer family, who, at least in England, have a proper coat of their own, Malcolm Storer, in his book *Annals of the Storer Family*, says that the confusion began when Charles Storer (b. 1761; d. 1821), son of Ebenezer Storer (1729–1807), wrote his name by chance on a bookplate belonging to a member of the Andrews family. A reproduction of the bookplate with Charles Storer's name is given and the plate is the same as the one believed to be by Hurd. This does not, however, explain the use of the arms by his grandfather Ebenezer (1699–1761), referred to above, and probably used by him thirty-eight years earlier.

Hurd, no doubt, was commissioned by one of the Storers to engrave the plate, leaving the name blank for members of the family to inscribe their signatures on a coat which they believed their own, and Charles naturally used it in that way, as did D. H. Storer later.

Apthorp, East

Eminent Episcopal clergyman, one time rector of Christ Church, Cambridge; born, 1733; married, a daughter of Foster Hutchinson; died, 1816.

[93   ]

Nathaniel Hurd's Bookplates

This unsigned plate in the Library at Dartmouth College strongly resembles Hurd's work. The plate resembles the one for Thomas Apthorp with the addition of a martlet above the millet dexter. The decoration is different and the scroll is empty, though Allen refers to a copy with the motto 'Nemo Nisi Christus' (Nothing unless Christ).

Arms: Per pale nebule arg. and az. 2 pierced mullets counterchanged. In dexter chief a martlet.

Crest: A mullet az.

Scroll: Empty.

Name: East Apthorp (italic caps), A.M. (script caps), Cambridge (script), MDCCLXI (Roman caps).

Style: Jacobean.

Signed: No signature

No. and [   ] above.

Allen No. 27. Dartmouth. Not in A.A.S.

APTHORP, STEPHEN

Probably of Massachusetts.

Arms: Per pale nebule arg. and az. 2 mullets pierced counterchanged. In sinister chief a fleur-de-lis arg.

Crest: A pierced mullet arg.

Scroll: Empty.

Name: Steph: Apthorp, in rather fine script.

Style: Chippendale. No border.

Signed: N Hurd Sc^p in script.

Printed in black and sepia.

APTHORP, THOMAS

Thomas Apthorp was born here in 1741 and died in England.

His unsigned plate in the Dartmouth College Collection appears to be designed by Hurd.

The arms and crest are identical with those of Stephen, with the exception of the omission of the fleur-de-lis. The decoration, though different in detail, is in Hurd's style with a wasp on the right of the plate.

Arms: Per pale nebule arg. and az. 2 mullets pierced counterchanged.

[94   ]

Nathaniel Hurd's Bookplates

Crest: A pierced mullet arg.
Motto: Juste Rem Para (Prepare the thing justly).
Name: In italic caps.
Style: Chippendale.
Signed: No signature.
          No. and [ ] below.
Allen No. 29. Dartmouth. Not in A.A.S.

ATKINSON, THEODORE

There were five in the Atkinson family of New Hampshire named in succession Theodore. The bookplate was probably engraved for the fourth or fifth Theodore. The latter was son of the Chief Justice;[1] born, 1736; Harvard College, 1757; married in 1762 Frances Deering, daughter of Samuel Wentworth, and died in 1769 without issue.

Mrs. Atkinson's portrait by Copley, painted in 1765, is owned by the New York Public Library.

The Chief Justice himself, for whom Allen thinks the plate was engraved, was born in 1697, Secretary of the Colony in 1741, Chief Justice and Delegate to Congress at Albany in 1754, and Major General in 1769, dying in 1779.

Arms: Vert a cross voided between 4 lions ramp. arg.
Crest: An eagle with wings raised proper or.
Motto: None.
Name: In script below.
Style: Chippendale with three-line border.
Signed: N Hurd Sc^p in script.
Allen No. 38.

ATKINSON, GEORGE

Same as above.

ATKINSON, HENRY

Same as above.

Note: A copy of the Atkinson plate was made and signed by Callender for William King Atkinson with a motto in scroll added.

---

[1] C. E. Goodspeed, in his *Angling in America*, quotes Brewster as saying, 'There was more silverware in his house than in any other house in New Hampshire.'

Nathaniel Hurd's Bookplates

BROWN, THOMAS

Harvard College, 1752; merchant; died, 1797.
These arms are much like those of Wentworth in Guillim and of Ace in the Choate pedigree.

Arms: On a chevron or between three leopards' faces three escallops.
Crest: An eagle's head couped.
Motto: En Esperance je vie (I live in hope).
Name: Tho.ˢ Brown, in script.
Style: Chippendale.
Signed: N Hurd Scᴰ, in script.
   Nᵒ and [   ] in left upper corner.
Allen No. 112.

CAMPBELL, JOHN

There were at least nine men of this name in the British Army at this time, several of whom were in the colonies from time to time, but as the records are incomplete in several particulars, it has been found impossible to be sure for which one Hurd designed this plate.

Owing to the fact that the arms show the cadency of the second son by the appearance of the crescent in the centre of the shield, it limits the selection to one who has a right to bear the arms and he would be a second son or the descendant of one.

There are two John Campbells who answer this description, but exact proof is lacking between them. The first is:

John Campbell (1753–1784), second son of John Campbell, Lord Stonefield; Lieut. in 7th Fusiliers May 9, 1774, and ordered to America; Capt. in 71st Reg., Dec. 2, 1775; Major in 74th Highlanders, Dec. 30, 1777; returned to England 1780; later distinguished himself in India.

The second, which appears more likely is:

John Campbell of the 22nd Regiment whose Lt. Col. was James Abercromby. This regiment was in Boston at the time of the Battle of Bunker's Hill and two of the companies, the Grenadiers, and light infantry under the command of Abercromby

[96   ]

were in the fight where Abercromby fell wounded, and died a few days later. John Campbell was promoted to succeed him with a higher rank, as is noted in Howe's Orderly Book on page 21 under date of July 24th which says

'22d (Gage's) Regiment. Major John Campbell to be Lt. Col. vice Abercromby, dead of his wounds.'

With the exception of the arms and crest, which are well known, the above-mentioned plate is almost like the one designed for John Murray, in the description of which will be found noted the elaborate treatment of trophies of war consisting of weapons and flags behind the shield, the bound captives, the Gorgon's head, and warlike implements. (See the Murray description.)

Arms: Quartered 1 and 4 Gyrony of 8 sa. and or (Campbell).
             2 az. a boar's head or couped and contourné.
             3 arg. a lymphad sa. without sails, flying 2 flags, the oars in action (Lorn).
             At the intersections of the quarters a crescent for difference (2d son).
Crest: A naked dexter hand grasping a short spear in bend sinister. (Tinctures unknown.)
Motto: In scroll below, Arma Parata Fero (I bear my arms ready).
Name: John Campbell Esqr in script with flourish.
Style: Chippendale.
Signed: N. Hurd Sculp Boston in italics at right.
           No. and [ ] at top.

This plate is in the collection at Dartmouth College. A copy was shown at the Museum of Fine Arts in 1904 and was described in the catalogue of that exhibition of early American engravers. Not in A.A.S.

CHANDLER, JOHN, JR.

A Loyalist of Worcester who took refuge in Boston in 1774 and embarked in 1776, dying in London in 1800. He was the grandfather of George Bancroft.

Arms: Chequy arg. and az. on a bend arg. three lions passant.
Crest: A pelican in her piety or.
Motto: None.

Nathaniel Hurd's Bookplates

Name: John Chandler Junr Esqr in script.
Style: Chippendale.
Signed: N. Hurd Sculp, in script.
Printed in black and red.
Allen states, on page 108, that this is 'without doubt the highest type of the Chippendale plate which Hurd made.'
Resembles the Hubbard plate.

CHANDLER, RUFUS

Brother of the above. Lawyer.
Same plate as John, Jr., printed in blue with first name changed.
Signed: N. Hurd Sculp, in script.
Allen No. 148.

CHILD, THOMAS

Possibly Thomas who was born in Barnstable in 1731, a son of Thomas and Mary Child; married Mary Freeman, 1772; moved to Portland in 1764; entered Government service, 1769; first Postmaster of Portland and in Custom House, where he continued until his death in 1787.

This is the same coat that was used by Sir Jonas Child, Bart., of Wanstead, Essex, England, though the connection to the American family has not been traced.

Arms: Gu. a chevron eng. erm. between three eagles close.
Crest: An eagle rising entwined by serpent.
Motto: Fari Aude (Dare to speak).
Name: Thomas Child, in script below.
Style: Chippendale.
Signed: No signature.

M.F.A. Catalogue of 1904 lists this plate without the motto, but signed 'N. Hurd Sculp,' and Finchem lists a plate with same signature. As the copy we have seen was unsigned, but with motto like Allen No. 160, there are probably two states to that plate.

COURTENAY, HENRY

Henry Courtenay of Massachusetts.
Arms: Two coats impaled.

Baron: Quartered.
           1 and 4 or three torteaux.
           2 and 3 or a lion ramp.
           At the intersection a crescent for difference.
Femme: Sable 2 bars erm. and in chief 3 crosses
           pattee arg.
Crest: A dolphin embowed.
Scroll: None.
Name: Henry Courtenay Esqr in script.
Style: Chippendale.
Signed: Not signed, but doubtless by Hurd.
Allen No. 184.

DANA, FRANCIS

Born in Charlestown, Massachusetts, 1743, son of Richard and Lydia Trowbridge Dana. Married, 1773, Elizabeth Ellery of Newport. Jurist and diplomat. Died 1811 in Cambridge after having been a delegate to the Continental Congress in 1778 and 1784 as well as Minister to Russia in 1785 (?) and Chief Justice of Massachusetts in 1791.

Arms: Or a chevron eng. gu. bet. three hinds trippant.
Crest: A fox passant.
Motto: Cavendo Tutus (Safe by caution). Engraved as one word.
Name: In script below.
Style: Chippendale.
Signed: N. H. Sc^p, in italics and script.
         No. and [   ] above.
Allen No. 201.

DANA, J. FREEMAN

Born, 1793; died, 1827. Chemist, taught at Dartmouth and College of Surgeons, New York.

Same plate with 'Francis' erased and 'J. Freeman' added with pen.

DANA, SAMUEL

Brother of James Freeman Dana and son of Luther Dana, Samuel's middle name being Luther. Born in Amherst, New Hampshire, in 1795; chemist by profession; d. 1868.

Signed: N. H. Sc⁰, in italics and script.

The same plate as Francis Dana with 'Francis' erased from plate and 'Samuel' written by pen. In the Vose Collection. Not in A.A.S.

DANA, RICHARD HENRY

Son of Francis, born, 1787; died, 1879. Poet, essayist, and critic. Harvard graduate, admitted to the bar in 1811; editor of *North American Review*; father of the author of *Two Years Before the Mast*. The same copper plate with the owner's name, the signature of Hurd and the letters N° in corner entirely erased. In place of the latter, A.D. 1569 is engraved, and also with 'Richard Henry Dana' engraved in script in place of the original owner's name.

Unsigned.

Allen, No. 202.

DANA, RICHARD HENRY

The same plate as the previous one of this name with the date and owner's name engraved with different script, and with the bracket, used for the number of the volume in the right upper corner erased from plate.

Unsigned.

DANA, EDMUND TROWBRIDGE

Translator, editor of works on International Law, son of R. H. Dana and grandson of Francis. Harvard Law School, 1841; died, 1869.

The same coat of arms as Francis, with all the old name erased from the plate, with new name printed in script, and the date A.D. 1569 in finer figures and in slightly different location in left upper corner.

Allen No. 200.

DANA

The same design re-engraved by another hand. The motto, which in earlier plates was engraved incorrectly in one word, is in this later plate spaced in two words. The name 'Dana' is engraved at bottom in Old English and the date A.D. 1569 is omitted.

PLATE XXII

Nathaniel Hurd's Bookplates

First state: Proof on yellow paper before addition of name.
Second state: Proof on thick glazed white paper with Dana engraved.
Third state: Finished print of bookplate.

DANFORTH

Probably the plate of Dr. Samuel Danforth, born, 1740; Harvard College, 1758; Boston physician and Loyalist, but remained in Boston after the siege. Fellow of the American Academy of Arts and Sciences; President of the Massachusetts Medical Society; died, 1827.

This coat is much like those of the Blake and Jones families (see *Heraldic Journal*), and on a tankard given in 1736 by Dr. Elijah Danforth to the First Church in Dorchester, made by Nathaniel Hurd's father Jacob.

Arms: In chief an eye and in base a lozenge az. In upper left above design a sun in splendor.
Crest: None, replaced by pile of three books.
Motto: Ubi plura nitent non ego paucis offendar maculis (I am not offended by a few spots).
Name: Danforth, in script.
Style: Chippendale.
Signed: N. H. Sc^p, in script.
Allen No. 203.

DeBlois, Lew

A careful examination of this plate will prove that the name is Lew and not Lew^s or Lewis, as it is frequently written. This name no doubt refers to Lewis DeBlois, since the plate is reputed to have been taken from a book inscribed 'Lewis de Blois his book Decr. 1749.'

He was a brother of George and a Loyalist and he died in England in 1779.

From the above evidence the plate must have been engraved when Hurd was not over nineteen and it naturally shows a crudeness as compared with his later work.

Arms: Three pales vair, on a chief or an eagle contourné.
Crest: Out of a marquis's coronet an eagle's head erased.

[101   ]

Nathaniel Hurd's Bookplates

Motto: None.
Style: Jacobean.
Name: Lew: DeBlois, script on a curtain.
Signed: Nathaniel Hurd Sculp, in script, in the space above the
curtain containing the name.
Allen No. 212.

DeBlois, George

Son of George and Elizabeth DeBlois; born at Oxford, 1739/40;
arrived in Boston, 1761; married his cousin Sarah in 1771, and
lived in Salem. An ardent Loyalist he fled to Halifax in 1775 and
returned to Boston in 1799, dying at Newport, Rhode Island, in
that same year.

The plate is similar to the one previously described with 'Lew'
erased and 'Geo' inserted in ink in its place.

Dering

There are at least six bookplates originally designed by Hurd
and used by the Dering family of Shelter Island, but of these
plates three were altered by others from the 1749 plate.

The earliest bookplate made in the colonies which is both
signed and dated is the one which Hurd engraved for Thomas
Dering, dated 1749. He engraved two others, however, which
from their workmanship are believed to be earlier, as follows:

Dering, Thomas 17

This plate is entirely different from the later plates and is more
of a paster or label. It consists of a one-and-one-half-inch circle
in double line, with a horizontal double line across it seven-eighths
inch from the top, and above it the Dering crest of a roebuck's
head couped or on a torse. Below, figures 17, followed by a blank
space for completing the year when the volume was purchased.
There is a little foliation about the ends of the line inside the circle.
The whole is very crude, but it is decidedly in Hurd's early manner,
though unsigned. Allen No. 220.

Dering, Thomas

Another Dering plate, believed to be before 1749, is an elaborate
armorial one done in a crude style. The only copy believed to be

Nathaniel Hurd's Bookplates

in existence was burned, though a photograph had been made. Lately, however, one of the original plates pasted in a copy of a book belonging to Thomas was secured by the Metropolitan Museum of New York. This copy shows the Dering arms and crest, described later, in a complicated Jacobean treatment with supporters of naked women holding spears and a dart, emerging from arabesques, supported on brackets resting on women's heads.

Under the left bracket is concealed the signature 'N Hurd,' and below on the right is the word 'Sculp,' both in italics.

Between the brackets appears an indistinct group which seems to have on the right a figure holding the staff of a flag with one hand and blowing a horn. On the left appears a hound held at collar by a small figure. A triangular decoration is partly indicated at lower right.

Below this is an empty ribbon and underneath that the name of Thomas Dering in heavy script. It is a labored design, but shows promise of his future work.

DERING, THOMAS

This plate, which is the earliest one referred to above as being both signed and dated, and which was drawn for the head of the family, must have been the third plate which Hurd made for Thomas.

This Thomas Dering was the son of Henry E. and Elizabeth Dering, born in Boston in 1720, and moved to Shelter Island on the death of his father Henry in 1750. Thomas married in 1756 Mary Sylvester of Newport and lived for a short time in Middletown, Connecticut. He died in 1785 leaving three children.

The arms are like those given in Guillim for Deering (note spelling) in 1664 and were confirmed to both Nicholas and Thomas, so that it seems probable that the family had a right to use them.

Arms: Gu. 3 roebucks' heads couped or.
Crest: On a torse a head of the field.
Motto: None.
Style: Chippendale.
Name: In script below.
Signed: N Hurd Sculp 1749, in script.
Allen No. 219. First state.

[103]

Nathaniel Hurd's Bookplates

DERING, HENRY P.

This second state of the plate was altered for Henry Parker Dering, born Shelter Island, 1763; Yale, 1784; died, 1822. It is the original Thomas plate last described, with 'Thomas' erased and 'Hen^y P.' re-engraved with both Hurd's signature and the date 1749 left in, and was used by Thomas Dering's son.

DERING, N. H.

This plate was for Dr. Nicoll H. Dering, son of General Sylvester Dering of Shelter Island and grandson of Thomas. He was born in 1794; Yale, 1813; and died at Utica in 1867.

This is the same plate engraved for Thomas, but with the 'Thomas' erased and 'N H' written by pen in place and crudely done.

DERING, NICOLL H.

This is also the same Thomas Dering plate, in the third state, but with name of owner, signature, and date completely erased from the plate and the new name re-engraved in modern script.

Note: There is also in A.A.S. a modern engraved plate copied closely after Hurd, with this full name in Old English, and added above the name, a motto without scroll — Sola Nobilitas Virtus (Virtue alone is Nobility).

DUMARESQ, PHILIP

The scion of an English family famous in the early annals of the Channel Isles. Their descendants engaged in trade, and the father of Philip of the same name was the first of the family to come to Boston and settle there on Hawley Street, after having served as a lieutenant in the Royal Navy. As owner of a ship he travelled in his voyages between the Isle of Jersey and Boston, dying about 1774.

The son Philip, for whom the plate was made, was born in Boston in 1737. After being educated in England, he returned to this country as aide-de-camp to Lord Dunmore. In 1773 he married Rebecca, a daughter of Dr. Sylvester Gardiner of Boston, and became one of the officers of old Trinity Church.

No copy of this plate is available for examination, so the exact description of the plate cannot be given, but as the design is said to be armorial and of Chippendale style, similar to the Courtenay plate, it probably contains the Dumaresq arms. Some of the present family use the arms impaled with others, but if the Hurd design is unimpaled, the description is probably as follows:

Arms: Gu. 3 escallops or, in chief a mullet for difference.

Crest: A bull passant guardant proper.

Motto: Dum viro spero (While I live, I hope) (probably omitted). Supporter: greyhounds rampant (probably omitted).

Signed: N. Hurd Sculp.

Allen No. 236. Not in A.A.S., though the Lichtenstein Collection is believed to contain a copy.

FOSTER, ISAAC

Captain Isaac Foster of Charlestown; Harvard College, 1758; portrait painted by Badger (?); died, 1781. His widow, Mary Russell Foster, was the second wife of Colonel John Hurd, second son of Jacob, whom she married in 1783. She was no relation to the Colonel's first wife by the same name.

These arms are identical, except for a green chevron, with the ones given in the Gore Roll for John Foster, 'Coll of the Livegard to the Earl of Bellomont, Gov. of Provins of Mass. Justice of Common Pleas of Suffolk Cy and on His Majesty's Council 1710.'

Arms: Arg. a chev. vert bet. three hunting horns sa. stringed gu.

Crest: An arm in armor embowed holding a broken tilting spear ppr.

Motto: Mille mali species mille salutis habeo (In a thousand evils I have a thousand chances of safety). Supporters: Dexter a dove, sinister a crane.

Name: Isaac Foster in script.

Style: Jacobean.

Signed: N. Hurd Sc^p in script.

The above is in black, but there is another impression in blue.

Allen No. 282.

FRENCH, JONATHAN

These arms appear in Guillim as those of French, of Thornadie or Thorndike of Scotland, and in this country of French of Newport, Rhode Island; of Braintree Manor, New York; and of Braintree, Massachusetts, though the record of their exact connection with the family in this country is not complete.

The plate of Jonathan French, though unsigned, is probably by Hurd, and was engraved for the son of Moses French of Braintree, the Reverend Jonathan French, born in Braintree, 1739; married Abigail Richards, 1773; ordained pastor of the South Church, Andover, 1772, 'a clergyman of great excellence and reputation,' and died in 1809.

> Arms: Arg. a chevron az. betw. three boars' heads erased.
> Crest: Surmounting a squire's helmet a torse and a fleur-de-lis argent.
> Motto: None. (In later prints, Tuebor, I will defend.)
> Name: Jonathan French, in script.
> Style: Jacobean.
> Unsigned.
> Allen No. 291.

GREEN, FRANCIS

Philanthropist and merchant, born, 1742, son of Benjamin and Margaret (Pierce) Green, and a descendant of Percival Green, who arrived in Boston in 1635, moving to Cambridge in 1636. Francis graduated from Harvard College in 1760; married Susannah Pierce in 1769; being a Loyalist he spent some years in Nova Scotia and England, returning to Medford in 1797, where he died in 1809.

His arms are to be found in Guillim, but are not in Miner Pedigree or Gore Roll, though they were used by the Green family in England in 1688.

> Arms: Arg. on a fess az. between three pellets charged each with a lion's head erased, a griffin passant between two escallops arg.
> Crest: A fir tree.
> Motto: Aestate Hyeme que Idem (In age and winter unchanged).
> Name: In script.
> Style: Chippendale.
> Signed: N. Hurd Sculp.

Nathaniel Hurd's Bookplates

Allen No. 323.

Note: This plate must not be confused with a modern copy of Hurd's engraving with 'Francis Cushing Green' in late script engraving at bottom, which is also in A.A.S.

GREENE, BENJAMIN

A wealthy Boston merchant, born, 1713; died, 1776; connected with the Rhode Island family. (See *The Greenes of Rhode Island*, 1903, p. 149.)

Copley's portrait of him was burned in the great Boston Fire of 1872.

These arms are like those of Benjamin Greene in Guillim and similar to those registered in the College of Heralds before 1600.

In the burying ground of King's Chapel on the Greene tomb appears the same coat, but with different crest.

Arms: Az. three stags trippant or.

Crest: A stag's head couped or.

Motto: Scroll empty.

Style: Jacobean.

Name: In script.

Signed: N = H Sc = p in roman script.

Allen No. 326.

A second state of this plate has the date 1757 added under the name. Allen No. 327.

GREENE, THOMAS

Brother of Benjamin Greene, born in Boston, 1705; Yale, 1727; died, 1763. A wealthy man, said to have owned the first coach in Boston, which had on it the Greene coat of arms. His portrait was painted by Copley and is owned by one of his descendants. (For further details see page 147 of *The Greenes of Rhode Island*.)

In the collection at Dartmouth College there is a small plate 1¾″ × 2½″) giving the same arms as Benjamin Greene just described, but omitting the helmet in the crest, the scroll, and substituting garlands of flowers instead of the decoration about the coat, the blazon being in an oval instead of a shield, as follows. The work resembles Hurd's.

Arms: Az. three stags trippant or.

Crest: A stag's head couped or.
Motto: No scroll or motto.
Style: Chippendale with wreath.
Name: In script.
Unsigned.
Not in A.A.S.

GREENE, THOMAS, JR.

Son of Thomas, born, 1729; died, 1766. (See page 246 of *The Greenes of Rhode Island.*)

This plate is referred to by Allen in No. 330, p. 211, as follows: 'Armorial Jacobean. Motto, Study to Know Thyself. Signed, N. Hurd Scp. Very similar to the plate of Benjamin Greene.'

Notwithstanding a search, no original copy of this has been found, though it is assumed that Allen has seen one.

In the collection of the A.A.S. there is a print of the Greene arms similar to the Benjamin Greene coat, and undoubtedly engraved from the latter by the artist. It is practically identical with that plate, except that it is a little smaller, has a different scroll with a motto in English, 'Study to know yourself.' The lower part of the original frame moulding has been erased and a new bottom to the frame engraved showing slightly different spacing.

It is evident that the plate has been cut off below the frame, thus omitting the name of the original owner and the signature. On the margin of the paper below the frame is written by pen the name of Wm. J. Potter, who was related to the Greene family. The 'J' in the signature was written as was the mode at one time 'J' in a way that resembles a 'T.'

This print bears every evidence of being by Hurd's hand and is believed to be from the altered Thomas Greene, Jr., copper. Possibly Allen copied the motto in error by substituting 'Thyself' for 'Yourself,' as the former was usually used.

GREENLEAF, WILLIAM

Merchant and zealous patriot of Boston, and one time Sheriff of Suffolk County; born, 1725; died, 1803.

Arms: Arg. a chev. between three leaves erect vert, on the chev. a martlet for difference.

Plate XXIII

Nathaniel Hurd's Bookplates

Crest: A dove holding in its bill an olive branch.
Motto: None.
Style: Chippendale.
Name: Script.
Signed: N Hurd Sc^p, in roman and script.
      N° above at left.
Allen No. 331.

GREENLEAF, WILLIAM, JUN^R

Probably the one who graduated from Harvard College in 1777 and died in 1778.

The same plate as above with 'Junr' added, first in script and engraved later after the name.

Signed as above.

HALE, ROBERT

Born in Beverly, 1703; Harvard College, 1721; physician in Beverly; at Louisburg with Pepperell in 1745; member of the State Legislature; Sheriff of Essex County in 1761; died in 1767.

These arms are recorded as borne by the Hale family of great antiquity in Kent, and still residing there in 1924, and the connection between the English family and the Beverly one seems to be complete.

Arms: Gu. three arrows points down.
Crest: A mailed arm embowed ppr. holding an arrow.
Motto: None.
Name: Robert Hale Esqr below, in script.
      OF BEVERLY in roman caps.
Style: Chippendale.
Signed: N. Hurd Sc^p, in italics.
Allen No. 339.

HARVARD COLLEGE

The history of the various seals and dies of Harvard University is extremely interesting, though hardly germane to this work; but if one wishes to know more about them, an article by Professor S. E. Morison in the *Harvard Graduates' Magazine* of September, 1933, will be found instructive.

The earliest design for a seal occurs as a very rough sketch in

[109   ]

Nathaniel Hurd's Bookplates

the Overseers' Records of 1643, showing three open books and the word 'Veritas' on a plain shield. Shortly afterward the chevron was added, and several seals were in existence before 1693, when John Coney, the silversmith, was paid £2–2–6 to design and cut a die for the seal. Though this die was lost, it was used by the College as late as 1795.

Professor Morison states in his article that

> On Dec. 12, 1765, the Corporation in adopting new Library laws declared, 'A print of the College Seal handsomely engraved, with a Blank Space to insert the Name of the Donor, shall be pasted in the beginning or End of Every Book.'

The first College bookplate engraved by Nathaniel Hurd in consequence of this vote, and the 'detur' bookplate by the same engraver, were obviously based on the 1650 seal, although the motto was taken from another and the word 'Veritas' was omitted. The field of the shield is hatched vertically, and as Hurd was an engraver of coats of arms, he might have intended these hatchings to represent red.

There were no hatchings on Coney's seal of 1693, but it is known that after the boat race of 1858, when Eliot and his crew wore red bandannas on their heads to distinguish the Harvard oarsmen, the College increasingly used crimson for its color, but did not adopt it officially until 1910.

'Detur' Seal

The earliest of these Hurd plates is in the form of a circular seal with the College Arms:

Gu. a chev. arg. between three open books.

Motto: Christo et Ecclesiae in a circle.

Surrounding circular inscription Sigill : Coll : Harvard : Cantab : Nov Angl : 1650, and enclosed in a holly wreath.

Above a scroll with Detur Digniori (Let it be given to the more worthy).

Signed: N — Hurd Sculp below, in centre.

Allen No. 351.

This plate was used in presentation copies to students.

Note: The word 'Veritas' does not appear on this plate, nor on

[110]

any of Hurd's, but was shown on a later engraving by another hand.

The remaining Harvard bookplates designed by Nathaniel are variants of the following, and are all signed 'N. Hurd Sc Boston' in italics.

In these and the other Harvard plates, which are meant to be used for books given to the Library, the Harvard circular seal appears at the top of the plate nearly like the 'Detur' design, with the motto, 'Christo et Ecclesle' (*sic*) in an incomplete circle.

The framework of the seal is embellished with garlands of fruit and flowers and is surmounted by three books resting on a support with a sun in splendor above all. Below the seal depends a large blank curtain with folds at side surmounted by globes on either hand, with a space on the curtain for an inscription by the giver, and signed below, 'N. Hurd Sc Boston.' This plate is printed in black and in red.

Allen No. 352.

Ex Dono

Same design as above, but with 'Ex Dono' engraved on the curtain and the word in the motto, 'Ecclesle,' corrected to 'Ecclesiae.'

Signed: N Hurd Sc Boston, in italics.

The Gift of

Same design with 'The Gift of' engraved in place of 'Ex Dono.'

Signed: N Hurd Sc Boston, in italics.

Hancock

Another plate of same design with 'Hancock' on the curtain to indicate the books given by Gov. John Hancock.

Signed: N Hurd Sc Boston, in italics.

Printed in black and in red.

Shapleigh

Same design, but with 'Shapleigh' on curtain.

Signed: N Hurd Sc Boston, in italics.

Printed in black and in red.

Nathaniel Hurd's Bookplates

Thorndike

Same design with 'Thorndike,' except that in the seal the word 'Ecclesiae' is spelled 'Ecclesle.'

Signed: N Hurd Sc Boston, in italics.

Printed in black only.

HOAR, RICHARD

The plate of Richard Hoar, about whom nothing has been discovered by the author, is a very fine piece of engraving, though it does not resemble Hurd's work enough except to be classed as extremely doubtful.

The A.A.S. copy that has been seen has a forged signature of 'Hurd Boston 1752' in ink directly under the scrolled border, a method of signing that does not exist in any other of Hurd's plates.

Nevertheless, as this plate has been included in other lists of Hurd's plates, it is mentioned here, though it is not believed by the author to be by Hurd's hand.

HOBBY, JONATHAN

Though no definite proof of ownership is at hand, the only contemporary of this name living near Boston who seems probable was one born at Reading, Massachusetts, on May 4, 1739, the son of the Reverend William Hobby. There is only one record pertaining to the son, which is that his father borrowed for him on August 29, 1761, the sum of one hundred pounds.

The arms on the plate were apparently taken by Hurd from Guillim, as they appear there under the name of Hoby, without a crest, which latter was presumably added, possibly as appropriate to the owner's interests. Whether Hobby had a right to the Hoby blazon must remain doubtful, but there was a Sir Charles Hobby, knighted in 1705 for good service done in New England for the Crown (*Heraldic Journal*, IV, 116), who left no direct descendants. He had a nephew, however, the Reverend William Hobby, born in Boston, 1701, died in Reading, 1765, the father of Jonathan, who had, therefore, some reason for adopting the arms as follows:

Arms: Three spindles, 2 and 1.

Crest: A ship of war under topsails, ensigns and pennants flying.

[112]

Nathaniel Hurd's Bookplates

Motto: Stud'y's et moribus (By zeal and by character).
Style: Chippendale.
Name: In script below.
Signed: N H, in roman; S^p, in script.
       N° and [   ] above crest.

HOLYOKE, EDWARD AUGUSTUS

Physician, born, 1728, in Marblehead, a descendant of Edward Holyoke, who emigrated from England in 1638, and a son of the Reverend Edward Holyoke who was President of Harvard from 1737 to 1769. Edward Augustus was twice married, performed an operation at the age of ninety-two years, and died in 1829, aged one hundred and one.

These arms appear in 1711 in the seal of Ebenezer Holyoke, and are on President Holyoke's teapot by Jacob Hurd presented to him on his second marriage in 1725, though the crest in this latter coat is a crescent.

Arms: Az. a chev. arg. cotised or between three crescents of the second.

Crest: A cubit arm vested holding in a sinister hand an oak branch vert fructed or.

Motto: Duce Natura Sequor (I follow the lead of Nature).

Name: In script below.

Style: Chippendale.

Unsigned.

Allen No. 385.

Note: The shield and decorations in Chippendale style strongly resemble Hurd's work. The name is certainly unlike script by Hurd, or if it is his, it must be a very early attempt at his bold flourishes. Marshall thinks the work more like Thomas Johnston.

HOOPER, JOSEPH

A Harvard graduate of this name of the class of 1763 may have been the owner of this plate.

These arms appear on a silver bowl made by Jacob Hurd and at one time owned in Newburyport, engraved H/RR (for Robert and Ruth Hooper).

Arms: Arg. on a fess vert between three boars passant or as many annulets of the first.

[113   ]

Crest: On a helmet a boar's head couped or.
Motto: Scroll empty.
Name: Below in script.
Style: Jacobean.
Signed: N. Hurd Sc^p, in italics.

HOOPER, STEPHEN

Same plate as above.
Signed: N. Hurd Sc^p, in italics.

HOOPER, WILLIAM

Born, 1742, a native of Boston, but a signer of the Declaration of Independence as a representative of North Carolina; married Anne Clark in 1767 and died in 1790.

Arms: Two coats impaled.

Baron: Or a crescent arg. on a chief az. two roses.
Femme: Arg. a bend sa. between two unicorns' heads erased or. On the bend three annulets arg.

Crest: A star of sixteen points.
Motto: Haec Etiam Parentibus (This also I owe to my ancestors).
Name: In script.
Style: Chippendale.
Signed: N. H. Sc^p, in italics.
Allen No. 388.

HUBBARD, WILLIAM

The arms are shown in Guillim for Thomas Hayes, of Bourne, England, in 1619, but it is probable that Hurd took these arms from the Hubbard tomb in the Copps Hill Burying Ground where Deacon Hubbard was buried. The arms on this tomb appear without crest or motto.

William Hubbard was probably one of the two great-grandsons of the first emigrant, also named William. They were both of Boston, one born, 1736, died, 1786 (son of John), the other a son of Daniel, 1739–1801, who also lived in Norwich, Connecticut, as well as Boston.

These arms and motto are still used in the family today:
Arms: Sable on a bend arg. three lions passant.

[114   ]

Nathaniel Hurd's Bookplates

Crest: On a cap of dignity az. turned up ermine a lion's head erased.

Motto: Nec Timeo Nec Sperno (I neither fear nor despise).

Style: Chippendale.

Name: Below in script.

Signed: N. Hurd sculp, in italics and script.

HURD

In the history of the Hurd family by Dena D. Hurd, the author definitely states that the arms of the Hurd, Heard, or Hord family date before 1300 and were granted in about the same form as is shown on this bookplate, but whether John Hord, the direct emigrant ancestor of Nathaniel, had the right to use the blazon is not definitely proved and might be questioned, as he was a 'Taylor.'

In any event, Nathaniel probably believed it to belong to his family and adopted it. These arms are:

Arms: Az. a lion rampant or on a chief arg. a crane proper between two mullets sa.

Crest: A raven sa. on a garb of wheat.

Name: Hurd in scroll.

Style: Chippendale.

Unsigned.

Allen No. 401.

This plate so definitely resembles Hurd's work that it is hardly presumptuous to attribute it to him, especially as there is no reason for any other engraver to have executed it.

There is no name engraved below the shield, but the copy owned by the American Antiquarian Society has 'Isaac Hurd's 1812' written below in ink by pen. Another copy seen by Allen has penned upon it 'Isaac Hurd's presented to Barzillai Frost.' There was a Dr. Isaac Hurd, a descendant from the original emigrant John Hord, a distant cousin of Jacob's, who was born in 1756, Harvard College, 1772. He was active in the Revolution and died in 1844. (See page 6.)

It may be well to mention here that the arms granted to the Hurds in England differed from those on the bookplate by having a helmet below the crest and the motto, 'Bona Bonis' (Good things to the good).

[115]

Allen states, 'The arms seem to be wholly imaginary, or at least borrowed from some other family,' but there seems to be no proof of this, as Burke mentions them.

Further discussion of the Hurd arms and an account of the actual grant to Jacob's heirs will be found in the text. (See page 84.)

JACKSON, JONATHAN

A Massachusetts merchant, statesman, and member of the Old Congress; born, 1743; died, 1810. (See *The Jacksons and the Lees*, edited by K. W. Porter, 1937.) His well-known pastel portrait by Copley is owned by Edward Jackson Holmes of Boston.

Arms: Az. four escallops argent, the field being divided into quarters by lines.

Crest: A covered urn takes the place of a crest.

Motto: Bona Quae Honesta (Good things and honest).

Name: Below, in script.

Style: Ribbon and wreath.

Signed: N. Hurd Sc^p, in script.

N^o and [ ] above.

Allen No. 419.

Note. An excellent modern copy of the Jonathan Jackson plate was made by F. C. Black for Charles Jackson whose name appears at the bottom. It is signed 'F C B after N. Hurd,' and is mentioned here only because the signature is so placed that it might be cut off without being noticed by an inexperienced collector and thus the plate be taken for an unsigned Hurd.

JARVIS, LEONARD, JUN^R

There were three persons bearing the name of Leonard Jarvis — father, son, and grandson — who might have been the owners of this plate, though for only the first two could it have been designed.

Leonard, the father, born, 1716, died, 1770, was a wealthy merchant with a prominent social position; Commissary of Supplies to British troops; First Colonel of the Cadet Corps, originally called the King's Guards, and later Independent Cadets; very loyal to his King, and a well-informed man of taste.

PLATE XXIV

Nathaniel Hurd's Bookplates

The son Leonard was born, 1742, became a merchant in high standing and was remarkable for his integrity. Due to the prohibition of trade with Boston, he moved to New Bedford. Returning later, however, he was appointed Inspector of Revenue by Washington and at one time Treasurer of Massachusetts. He lost most of his fortune in the Georgia Land Speculation, moved to Maine, and died in 1813.

Leonard, the grandson, who might have owned the plate by inheritance, was born in 1782, Harvard College, 1800, a man of high culture who filled various State offices, was a Member of Congress for two terms, United States Navy agent at Boston, and died in 1854.

The plate may have been engraved for the oldest of the three, and later 'Junr' was evidently added to the plate, and it could have been used by all three.

Arms: Arg. a chev. erm. between three birds or.

Crest: A demi-eagle or.

Motto: None.

Name: In large script.

Style: Chippendale (like Atkinson plate).

Signed: N. Hurd S^p, in italics.

Note: See *Ex Libris*, Washington, 1896–97, p. 78 (Widener Library). An original copy of this has not been located, though one was in the collection of James Duncan of London in 1896. Not in A.A.S.

JENKINS, LEWIS

The same plate as Robert with first name erased and 'Lewis' added by pen.

JENKINS, MARY

The same plate as Robert, described below, with first name erased and 'Mary' added by pen.

JENKINS, ROBERT

Of Boston. One of the subscribers for the chime of bells made in England for the steeple of Christ Church. His name as Warden and date of 1744 appear on the sixth bell.

Nathaniel Hurd's Bookplates

This plate is one of the finest and most elaborate engraved by Hurd, and is described as follows:

Arms: Two coats impaled.

     Baron: Quartered.

        1. Or a lion rampant regardant sable.

        2 and 3. Sable a chevron between 3 fleur-de-lis arg.

        4. Gu. two chevrons arg.

     Femme: Gu. a chev. erm. between three garbs.

Crest: An arm emb. in armor, a ribbon at the elbow, the naked hand grasping a sword.

Motto: Non reverter invitus (Reluctantly I return not). Below, a ship under sail.

Adjuncts: Two turbaned women arising out of scrolls.

Name: Robert Jenkins Sen[r], in script (Sen[r] by pen).

Style: Jacobean.

Signed: N. Hurd, in italics.

Allen No. 429.

Note: Some copies are dated 1751 in pen.

LIVINGSTON, PETER R.

Of the prominent New York family whose great estate was at Livingston Manor on the Hudson.

Peter of Clermont was a son of Robert (died, 1790) and a brother-in-law to William Smith Livingston and was born in 1739 and married Margaret Livingston, his cousin, in 1758. He was a member of the New York Assembly and a leader of the Whigs of New York, dying in 1794.

The arms are those of the Livingston family, all of whose prominent members used the blazon with slight variations. The coat is not like the one in Guillim and no doubt Hurd got his design from the other family plates and made a remarkably fine engraving of it.

Arms: Quart. 1 and 4: Arg. 3 gilly flowers gu. within a double tressure flory counter flory vert.

   2d quart. 1 and 4: gu. on a chev. arg. a rose of the field bet. 2 martlets.

   Quart. 2 and 3: Az. 3 martlets or.

   3d quart. sa. a bend bet. 6 billets arg.

Nathaniel Hurd's Bookplates

Crest: A ship of 3 masts foretopsail set.
Motto: Prestat opes sapientia (Wisdom excels wealth).
Style: Jacobean in a thin oblong engraved frame with rope moulding between two lines.
Signed: N. Hurd Sc^p, in italics.
No. and [ ] above.
Allen No. 497, but not in A.A.S.

LIVINGSTON, PETER WILLIAM
Exactly the same plate with 'Peter R.' erased and 'Peter W^m' written in ink by hand, with motto re-engraved to Spero Meliora (I hope for the best).
(See *Ex Libris Journal*, London, p. 81.)
Dartmouth College Collection, but not in A.A.S.

LORING, JOHN J.
Allen states that this plate is 'undoubtedly' by Hurd, but this in the author's opinion is questionable. Although the mantling design is almost exactly like the Thomas Dering plate, the execution is less sure and is fainter. The script in the name is very different from Hurd's bold touch and must be by another hand and a later one.
Arms: Quartered arg. and gu. a bend engrailed az.
Crest: From a bowl az. five quills erect pur.
Motto: None.
Name: In late script.
Style: Chippendale.
Unsigned.

LOWELL, JOHN
Only son of the Reverend John Lowell, born at Newburyport, 1743; legislator and jurist, member of the Old Congress; died, 1802.
The arms of this family similar to those here described are recorded as early as 1573 in the Harleian MSS. in the British Museum.
Arms: Or a hand couped grasping 3 darts points down.
Crest: An urn in place of a crest.
Motto: Occasionem Cognosce (Perceive the opportunity).
Name: In script below.

[119]

Style: Chippendale decoration.
Signed: N. Hurd Sc^p, in script.
      No. [   ] beside crest.
Allen No. 520.

MARCHANT, HENRY

Born, 1741, in Martha's Vineyard, son of Hexford Marchant; married Rebecca Cooke, 1765; jurist, Attorney General of Rhode Island in 1770, delegate to the Continental Congress, 1777–1780 and 1783–1784; died, 1796.

These arms do not appear in Guillim, nor in the Gore Roll or the Mincr Pedigree, but they are found on the Bowdoin tomb in Copps Hill Burying Ground, excepting that the latter has a pelican crest.

Arms: Az. a chevron or between 3 owls.
Crest: From a ducal coronet a bird's claw couped.
Motto: Patria Cara Carior Libertas (Dear is country, dearer Liberty).
Name: In script.
Style: Chippendale.
Signed: N. H. Sc., in script.
This plate appears in black and in blue.

MARSTON, JOHN

A man of this name in 1752 kept a tavern named the Golden Ball located in Merchants' Row near the Dock.

Arms: Az. a chev. embattled arg. betw. 3 crowned lions' heads erased or.
Crest: A crowned lion's head erased or.
Motto: Scroll empty.
Name: Below, in script.
Style: Chippendale.
Signed: N. Hurd Sculp, in script.
Allen No. 556.
This plate is printed in black and red.
This coat appears in Guillim, though under a different name.

[120   ]

Nathaniel Hurd's Bookplates

MILLER, JOSEPH

As similar arms appear on a tankard once owned by Samuel Miller, of Rehoboth and Milton, it may well be that Joseph was of the same family.

Perhaps also the plate marked 'Jo Miller,' below described, may be that of Josiah who was born in Rehoboth in 1744; married Jemima Whipple in 1766, and fought in the Revolution.

Arms: Ermine, a fess or between 3 wolves' heads erased gu.
Crest: A wolf's head as in the arms.
Motto: Semper Paretus (Ever ready).
Name: Joseph Miller, in script with flourish.
Style: Chippendale.
Signed: N. Hurd Boston, in italics.

These arms were granted May 16, 1672.

MILLER, JO

Whether this plate was engraved for Josiah or Joseph Miller is not clear, but it is entirely different in design from the latter and is as follows:

Arms: Arg. a double tressure flowered and counter flowered az. over all a fess battled and counter battled gu.
Crest: A mailed arm embowed proper the hand grasping a dagger.
Motto: Post Tot Nauf Ragia Portum (Lo the harbor after so many disasters).
Name: In large script.
Style: Chippendale.
Signed: N Hurd Sc\u1d56, in script.

MURRAY, JOHN

Colonel John Murray, of Rutland, Loyalist, who fled to Boston in 1774 and left with the British army in 1776, dying at St. John in 1794.

With the exception of the name, arms, and crest, this plate is almost like that of John Campbell (see description). The embellishment of the two plates is by far the most elaborate of any of Hurd's bookplates, with its stack of arms, captives, etc.

The shield with a coat of arms appears to be resting on a balustrade. Behind the shield are flags, spears, guns, and other trophies of war. Below the shield is a Gorgon's head on an escutcheon, and on either side of this, a bound captive, one seated on a cannon and one standing. Beside these at right and left are a mortar and a powder barrel with pyramid of balls.

The difference between the Campbell and Murray plates is the embellishment, which appears to be reversed, and the latter has a background with tents and a fort, whereas the Campbell has no background. The neat pile of cannon balls in the foreground of the Murray has been scattered in the Campbell, and the barrel is replaced by a drum with a sword resting upon it, while the mortar by the balustrade is replaced by a pair of kettledrums.

The trophies are changed in detail, but the treatments are much alike.

Arms: On a field az. a lion rampant langued or.
Crest: A lion's head erased or.
Motto: None.
Name: In script below, with flourishes.
Style: Chippendale with martial trophies.
Signed: N. Hurd Scp^t, in italics.

NEWTON, LUCRETIA E.

This is undoubtedly the bookplate by Hurd of John C. Williams, with the name erased and the signature cut off the paper, and the name 'Lucretia E. Newton' printed from Old English type under the shield.

As Allen aptly states, 'An unwarrantable proceeding.'

For description of arms see the Williams plate.

OLIVER, ANDREW

This plate resembles Hurd's work and has been attributed often to him, but the detail is so nearly identical with the plate engraved for Gardiner Chandler and signed by P. Revere that there can be little doubt the Oliver plate was executed by the same hand. There is the possibility that, owing to Revere's many interests, he might have employed Hurd to work for him at times.

OSBORNE, SAMUEL AND PETER

Samuel Osborne was of Boston, and Allen, No. 628, states that he was a brother of Captain Jeremiah Osborne, who died at sea in 1768.

[122   ]

Nathaniel Hurd's Bookplates

Only one copy of this plate is known, and this, in 1894, was in the Mauran Deats Collection, but later changed hands and has not been located by the author.

The only description that can be stated now is that the plate is an armorial one of early Chippendale design with an empty wreath ribbon, and that it is signed N. Hurd Scp. (Fincham).

The American Antiquarian Society has a photographic reprint of a creased and damaged Peter Osborne plate which might possibly be by Hurd, and the coat on this is:

Arms: Arg. a bend sable between two lions rampant.

Crest: A crowned lion's head erased.

This may be like the arms on the Samuel Osborne plate, but it is merely supposition. Allen states that Peter Osborne was of Philadelphia.

In Guillim this coat is of Sir John Osborn, of Chicksands in Bedfordshire. No date given.

PACE, HENRY

Nothing has been found as to the derivation of the arms, and as for Henry Pace himself we only know that on June 8, 1770, he bought land and a house on Prince Street, Boston, from Thomas Greenough, and on the following 6th of July he sold the property to Ann Moore, spinster.

Arms: A chevron sable between three thistles in bloom.

Crest: A boar's head couped pierced in the neck by a crosslet fitché point to dexter.

Motto: Fortuna Favit Fortibus (Fortune favors the brave).

Name: Below, in script.

Style: Jacobean.

Signed: N. Hurd sc^p, in script.

PAGE, SAMUEL

This plate is unlike any of Hurd's in design, for it is merely a label and has no arms, but in the execution of the engraving and of the scrolls and garlands, it very strongly resembles Hurd's work.

The design consists of a Chippendale frame with 'The property of' in Roman letters in a small motto scroll above, and the name Samuel Page in script in the blank space left for the owner's name.

Unsigned.

[123   ]

PALMER, THOMAS

Overseer of the Poor in Boston, 1707–1708. Subscribed to Prince's *History*, 1736.

Arms: Two coats impaled.

        Baron: Arg. two bars and chief a running greyhound sa. on the bars three (2 . 1) trefoils arg.

        Femme: Quartered.

            1. Or a lion ramp.

            2. Arg. a naked arm issuing fesswise from the sinister flank, the hand holding a heart.

            3. Az. a boar's head couped.

            4. Or a galley with six oars raised and crossed in saltire, on the stern a flag.

Crest: A sitting greyhound or.

Motto: Vix ea Nostra voco (Hardly do I call these things ours).

Name: In script.

Style: Jacobean.

Signed: N. Hurd, in roman; Sculp., in script.

        No [ ] above.

PHILLIPS, JOHN

The founder of the Academy of his name at Exeter and the benefactor of the one at Andover, John Phillips, LL.D., was born in 1719, being the second son of the Reverend Samuel, Jr., and Hannah (White) Phillips, of Andover, Massachusetts.

John Phillips was a scholar, a philanthropist, and a successful man, dying in 1795 after a life of great influence.

The arms of the Phillips family appear as No. 63 in the Gore Roll, and differ only from those shown on Hurd's plate in having for a crest a lion rampant instead of a lion sejant, with a field argent instead of or.

The arms noted in the Gore Roll were borne by 'Samuel Phillips of Boston in ye cont. of Suffolk 1721.' This Samuel was born in Salem in 1690 and was the grandfather of John the Founder.

This coat of arms also appears as No. 982 in the 'Promptuarian Armorum,' and with slight variation in arms of different members of the family, including Christopher Phillips, of Norfolk County,

[124]

PLATE XXV

John Chandler Junr. Esqr.

N. Hurd Sculp.

Henry Courtenay Esqr.

Isaac Hurd

1812

Robert Jenkins Senr.

England, who was born about 1593. The right of this Phillips family branch to bear arms thus seems well demonstrated.

The bookplate of John Phillips, which appears in his old Preaching Bible at Andover, Massachusetts, is:

Arms: Or a lion rampant sa. chained and gorged.
Crest: A lion sejant sa. chained and gorged.
Motto: None, and no scroll.
Name: John Phillips engraved in script on plate. 'Esq.' added later with pen. Also added below, with pen, 'of Exeter 1775.'
Style: Chippendale with fine rope moulding border.

Unsigned, though doubtless by Hurd.

Not in A.A.S., but at Phillips Academy, Exeter, and the Metropolitan Museum of Art.

Allen No. 674.

PHILLIPS ACADEMY

The following statement made by a former librarian explains the derivation of the Academy bookplate:

> The Phillips Exeter Academy bookplate was made from that originally used by John Phillips, the founder of the Academy. The original plate is dated 1775, and, although unsigned, is probably the work of Nathaniel Hurd, of Boston. When the plate was adopted for the use of the school, the name John Phillips was erased and 'In usum Acadaemiae Phillipsiae Exoniensis' (For the use of Phillips Exeter Academy) put in its place, while above the crest was placed the motto, 'Pia mente studeatur' (Let it be studied with pious mind).

Other than the change listed above, the Academy plate is like that of John Phillips and bears the same coat of arms as is described for the founder previously given.

Allen No. 674.

POTTER, WILLIAM J.
See Thomas Greene, Jr.

[125   ]

Nathaniel Hurd's Bookplates

Born, 1728; notary public; confidential secretary of several Governors before the Revolution; Clerk of Courts of Common Pleas and Sessions in Suffolk County. In 1760, Hurd occupied a part of the building in which Price had his office. Price died in 1802.

Arms: A lion rampant regardant.
Crest: A pelican in piety or.
Motto: None.
Name: In script, below.
Style: Chippendale.
Unsigned, but undoubtedly by Hurd.
     N° and [   ] above crest.
Allen No. 700.

As there were three of this name who graduated from Harvard within a few years of each other, it is difficult to place this particular Nathaniel.

There was a Samuel Rogers, a Loyalist, of this period who sealed with these arms on a letter in 1751 and who was probably related to Nathaniel.

Arms: Arg. a chev. between three stags courant sa.
Crest: A stag trippant sa.
Motto: Ad Astra per Aspera (To the stars through trials).
Name: In script below.
Style: Jacobean.
Signed: N H Sc^p in italics.
     No. and [   ] above crest.
In Guillim this coat is borne by Edw. Rogers, D.D., Oxon; died, 1684.

THOMAS GRAINGER . SEXTON

Owing to the fact that there is a period on the plate between the names Grainger and Sexton, the question has arisen whether this is the bookplate of one named Sexton or of Thomas Grainger who was a sexton.

Mr. John T. Loomis, whose article in *Ex Libris* of Washington

[126   ]

Nathaniel Hurd's Bookplates

in 1896 first brought the matter to attention, felt that the plate was done for one Thomas Grainger, a son of Samuel Grainger, whose name occurs in the Report of the Record Commissioners under date of '1719, Jan^{ry} 25 Sam^{ll} Granger admitted, Ob. Proctor & George Shore, being his Suretys.'

> At a meeting of the Sel. men 27th of Jan^{ry}. 1719. Voted. That m^r Sam^{ll} Granger (according to his request) be admitted to keep School to teach writeing, Logick & Merchants Acco^{ts} in this Town he giveing Security upon his admittance as an Inhabit^t.

He must have died about 1732, for on January 16, 1733, there is an entry in the Record Commissioners' book as follows:

> Messrs. Boutineau and Johonnot with others applying to us, On acco^t of the School lately under the care of Mr. Samuel Grainger Deceased, which is become vacant by the Death of Mr. Grainger. And his Son Thomas Grainger being some time Usher to his Father who had Several Boarders, desire, That his Son Thomas Grainger may have Leave to carry on the School for Three Months under the Inspection of Mr. Andrew Le Mercier.
>
> Voted, that upon Condition Mr. LeMercier takes the Oversight of the School, that Mr. Grainger have Liberty to Instruct the Youth for Three Months.

Now it would appear from this and from the fact that Samuel Grainger's inventory contained £105–14 for books which Thomas presumably inherited, he could have had Hurd later design a bookplate for his library which at that figure was not inconsiderable.

As it was not infrequent that a bookplate was designed in a humorous spirit, though Hurd had never done so, and as a sexton might be supposed to 'usher' souls into the next world, the angels' wings and the motto, which meant 'Death is the door to Life,' would seem to be entirely appropriate, particularly as in those days middle names were not in vogue, so that Loomis and others believe this plate was made for Grainger, who was an usher or sexton, and it must be admitted that the case is well made out and may even be correct.

[127   ]

Nathaniel Hurd's Bookplates

On the other hand, it seems from further research that Thomas was only a minor when his father died, as noted in the bond of his guardian, which states he was 'about fourteen years,' and it is difficult to imagine him to be carrying on a school, unless the phrase 'about fourteen years' is not to be taken literally, and he might be older.

Further and final inventories, however, show that Samuel was insolvent when he died and that in his assets and, even allowing for his books, his 'spinet' and '4 base viols' with some broken instruments, as well as '2 pr. andirons and 4 negroes,' he could only muster £507–10 to settle £1076–2–3 of debts.

The library for which Thomas is supposed to have had the plate made must have disappeared, and therefore Mr. Loomis's theory rather falls to the ground, though without definite or final proof.

It has not been possible to attribute this bookplate to any particular man at present, but if it is possible that the period on the plate was merely a trifling defect and not meant for a punctuation mark, we should then ascribe the plate to the Sexton family whose arms it bears.

There was a Thomas Sexton of Boston who died in 1679 and who left nine children, one of whom may have been named after his father, who left a fairly large estate, among other items being noted a silver tankard, a caudle cup, some silver spoons, fourteen pewter porringers, as well as a negro girl, etc.

It is felt that the chances are, if time could be spent upon it, this bookplate would prove to belong to one of the Sexton family.

Arms: Three wings erect, two and one.
Crest: Out of a coronet a demi-winged horse or.
Motto: Mors Ianva Vita (Death is the door to life).
Name: Tho.⁵ Grainger . Sexton, in small script.
Style: Jacobean with voluminous scrolls about crest.
Signed: N:Hurd Sc., in roman and script.
Not in A.A.S.

SIMPSON, JONATHAN

The arms on the Simpson plate are given in Guillim as those of the paternal family of John Sympson of the Inner Temple, Judge

Nathaniel Hurd's Bookplates

of the Sherriffs' Court, and a descendant of the ancient family of Sympson of the North. The same coat belonged to the Simpsons of Scotland, but whether this particular Jonathan was of either of these families has not been traced.

Arms: Arg. on a chief vert three crescents arg.
Crest: A hawk rising or.
Motto: Lege et Intellige (Law and Reason).
Name: Below, in script.
Style: Chippendale.
Unsigned.
Allen No. 783.

Though the plate is not signed, it bears very strong characteristics of Hurd's hand, and even though the script is only partly distinctive, the plate is most probably his. Prints exist in black, blue, and green.

SMITH, WILLIAM

There are six of this name contemporary with Hurd, so the owner cannot be ascertained with certainty.

Arms: Or a chevron cotised sa. between 3 demi-griffins rampant couped sa. (two in chief combatant.) on the chevron a martlet arg. for difference.
Crest: An elephant's head erased or, charged on the neck with three fleur-de-lis az. 2 and 1.
Motto: Chacun à son gout (Each to his taste).
Name: In script, beneath.
Style: Chippendale.
Unsigned, but undoubtedly by Hurd.
Allen No. 803 and in A.A.S.

SMITH, SAMUEL

Of this name, too, we find three of Hurd's contemporaries, but cannot definitely place the right owner. This is the second state of the William Smith plate, with the first name erased from the plate and 'Samuel' re-engraved thereon, and the color of the griffins worn.

In M.M.A. and also in A.A.S.

Nathaniel Hurd's Bookplates

SPOONER, JOSHUA

Born, 1722; married Freelove Westcott; house carpenter by trade, and lived in Middleboro and Providence. Deputy to General Assembly in 1760; died, 1772.

Arms:　Vert a boar's head couped or.
Crest:　A boar's head pierced by an arrow, point to sinister.
Motto: Follow Reason.
Name:　In script below.
Style:　Jacobean, with diapered background, supporters and scrolls.
Signed: N. Hurd, in roman; Sc^t, in script.

Note: There are two examples of this plate, one with the name 'Joshua' written in before Spooner and the other with 'John J.' so written.

STORER

The bookplate which Hurd designed for the Storer family and no doubt drew under their direction, though unsigned, contained in reality the Andrews arms, and a complete description of this will be found under the caption 'Andrews.'

TRACEY, NATHANIEL

Born in old Newbury, 1751, philanthropist and patriot, and one of the financiers of the Revolution; oldest son of Captain Patrick Tracey, who had emigrated as a youth from Ireland. Nathaniel was one of those merchant princes whose romantic fortunes and extraordinary idiosyncrasies cast a glamour over the history of the ancient town of Newburyport.

He had a passion for acquiring fine houses. His purchases, it is said, extended along the whole Atlantic coast as far as Philadelphia. Among others he bought the John Vassall mansion in Cambridge.

> But he flew his financial kite too high. His seven score merchantmen and cruising ships were wrecked or captured, his huge Government contracts were repudiated, and in a few years he conveyed his property for the benefit of his creditors. (*Henry Vassall*, p. 57, by Batchelder.)

[　130　]

Arms: Or between 2 bends gu. an escallop — bendwise in chief.

Crest: On a cap of dignity vert turned up ermine an escallop between two wings.

Motto: Scroll empty.

Name: Below in script.

Style: Chippendale.

Signed: N. H. Sc^p, in script.

TYLER, ANDREW

The well-known silversmith of Boston, 1692–1741, who married Miriam Peperell, was a Scavenger, Fire Warden, 1720–1727, Selectman, 1729–1732, and a member of the Brattle Square Church.

This coat could not have been used by Andrew, for it was not granted until 1774 by the College of Arms, and was recorded in 1778 by Tyler's daughter Catherine, Lady Heard, and was for use by Andrew, his brother William and their descendants. The plate must have been engraved between 1774 and 1777, and, though slightly different from the grant, is one of Hurd's finest engravings. (See *Heraldic Joural*, V, 3, p. 83.)

Arms: Gu. on a fess bet. 3 mountain cats pass. or a cross moline enclosed by 2 crescents of the field.

Crest: A demi-mountain cat rampant or charged on the shoulder with a cross crosslet fitché springing from a crescent gu.

Motto: Omitted.

Signed: N H Sculp, in italics.

The shield is on a diapered lining and supported on a mask and surrounded by elaborate scrolls with festoons of cloth depending therefrom in best Jacobean style.

VASSALL, HENRY

This descendant of a famous family, long resident in the West Indies, was born on Christmas Day, 1721, the fourteenth of eighteen children. He lived on the great family estate in Jamaica until 1740, when, attracted by the social and educational advantages of Boston, he moved there and settled in Cambridge,

Nathaniel Hurd's Bookplates

where he purchased a fine old mansion in which he lived in princely style.

In 1742, he married Penelope, daughter of the very wealthy Isaac Royall, who was born on her father's plantation in Antigua, and who had inherited one-half his wealth in 1739.

Henry did not attend college, but was a man of breeding, an officer, and an acknowledged leader. His title of Colonel was obtained from his position of Lieutenant-Colonel in the First Regiment of Middlesex Militia. His lavish expenditure and extravagant habits led him into financial difficulties as early as 1744 and plunged him into debt until his early death in 1769, leaving an estate so much involved that his family never recovered financially.

Arms: Az. in chief a sun in splendor. In base a chalice or.
Crest: A full-rigged ship, sails furled, ensign and pennants flying.
Motto: None.
Name: In script, below.
Signed: N: Hurd Sc\ᴰ, in script.
Style: Chippendale in rectangular frame.

Printed in black and in blue. Copy reproduced in Batchelder's book on Henry Vassall. Not in A.A.S.

The Vassall arms are also found on some of their silver which has been recovered, notably a cream jug by Jacob Hurd, #115, owned by the author, and two cans #79 and #80. (See pages 35 and 37, 38, of this volume.)

Note: By reversing the usual heraldic order of description this blazon might be considered a play upon the name Vassall.

Vase — Sol = Vassall

Arms: In base a vase or.
In chief sol in splendor.
Crest: A vessel.

VASSALL, JOHN, ESQ.

An older brother of Henry Vassall, born in 1713 in the West Indies, brought up on the plantation in Jamaica until he went to Harvard, from which he graduated in 1732. He was wealthy and not extravagant like his brother Henry from whom he bought, to

PLATE XXVI

Jonathan Jackson

Peter Wm Livingston

Henry Marchant

Joseph Miller

relieve Henry of embarrassment, an estate in Jamaica. Some of the proceeds of this sale went to pay a very large tailor's bill about which there was a considerable dispute later.

John was married twice, once in 1734 to Lucy, daughter of Lieutenant-Governor Spencer Phipps, and later to Lucy Barran, of Chelmsford. He left four children, of whom one was a son John, Harvard, 1757, who built Craigie House in Cambridge.

The elder John bore the title of Colonel and died young in 1747. It is said that there were sixty-eight of this family's name in and about Boston, but since the Revolution the name has vanished, except for the epitaphs on their tombs, due largely to their being Loyalists. Some of their silver with the family coat of arms has recently been found and has passed into the hands of collectors or museums.

The coat of John Vassall is, with the exception of the name and crest, exactly like that of Henry previously described. John Vassall's crest, instead of a full-rigged ship with sails furled and ensign and pennants flying, has a vessel with three lower masts only, with three small swallowtail pennants at the mast heads and an ensign from a staff at the poop. The embellishment about the shield is Chippendale, but slightly different in detail. There is no frame and the plate has 'Esqr' after the name, whereas this title is omitted in Henry's coat. It is, though unsigned, undoubtedly by Hurd. The plate occurs in three states, i.e.:

1. Without shaded background.
2. With shaded background in black and in blue.
3. Engraved with British flag at poop of ship in crest.

Allen No. 888.

WALKER, EDWARD

These arms are like those of Thomas Walker, of the Inner Temple, who descended from an ancient family with the same arms. They also appear on a silver brazier, dated 1715, made by Jacob Hurd, owned by Mrs. Paul Hamlen, from which, no doubt, Nathaniel took them for the plate, though he has omitted the branch in the canton's dove.

This, however, may be the plate for one Edward Walker, who graduated from Harvard in 1757 and died in 1801, but of whose life details are lacking.

The design and execution of this plate are very distinctly those of Hurd and it is probably by his hand.

Arms: Arg. a chevron between three crescents sa. on a canton sa. a dove arg.

Crest: A dove ppr. holding an olive branch in his beak.

Motto: None.

Name: In script, below.

Style: Chippendale.

Unsigned.

N° and [ ] above crest and frame about plate.

WENTWORTH

These arms are those given in Guillim as used by Baron Strafford Wentworth, K.G., and others of that family in England. In America they appear on the seals of Samuel Wentworth, of Portsmouth, and on that of Governor Benning Wentworth in 1743, and had been used by Sir John, the last Royal Governor of New Hampshire, born in Portsmouth, 1737, died, 1800; and by John, John 3d, and Paul of that family.

Hurd engraved two copper plates for the Wentworths, each different in its decoration, but with the same arms and motto, though quite different scrolls, one of which passes through the water falling from the shell at the bottom.

This latter plate is labelled 'Wentworth' in script, with space for a first name, while the other plate has no shell, but with the name 'Wentworth' in about the middle of the plate. Both plates are signed, the former having 'N. Hurd Sc^p' and the latter 'N Hurd Sculp,' both in script.

Arms: Sa. a chev. or between three leopards' faces arg.

Crest: A griffin passant.

Motto: En Dieu est Tout (In God is all).

Name: In script at right.

Style: Chippendale with a frame.

Signed: N. Hurd Sc^p, in script. (As above.)

Allen No. 922.

WENTWORTH, JOHN

Same plate (Wentworth at right), with 'John' added by pen before name.

[134]

Nathaniel Hurd's Bookplates

JOHN 3D

Same as above with 'John' added in front and 'ter' after the name.

Note: Copley drew a pastel about 1769 of a John Wentworth, born, 1737; died, 1820.

PAUL, GENT

This plate is the one without the shell and has engraved on plate 'Paul Wentworth, Gent,' in script.

Signed: N Hurd Sculp, in script.

This is possibly that Paul Wentworth who, born in America, had been Colonial Agent in England for New Hampshire, and had remained loyal to the Crown.

With a salary, an expense account, promises of a baronetcy, a seat in Parliament, and a sinecure, he superintended the work of other secret agents who wove a fantastic net about Franklin, when he was in Paris during the Revolution. Wentworth made frequent trips between London and Paris and it was he who persuaded Edward Bancroft to become a spy. (Van Doren's *Franklin*, p. 580.)

PAUL

Second state of above with 'Gent' erased. Signed as above, and with Nº [   ] above crest.

Note: The arms are very like those of Gee in Choate Pedigree.

The A.A.S. has a sepia plate of different Jacobean design and excellent execution which appears to be by Hurd, though the lower part has been mutilated by being cut off, leaving only the lower scroll of the motto ribbon which bears the name of Wentworth. The two missing scrolls might have contained the words 'By the' and 'Name of.'

The arms are of that family, i.e. sable, a chevron or betw. 3 leopards' faces arg. The crest, however, is slightly different, being a griffin statant with crown collar about neck surmounting a knight's helmet full-faced and open.

[135   ]

WILLIAMS, HENRY

This plate bears every indication of Hurd's engraving. The decoration is about like that on the signed Marston plate. None of this name being found, it is not yet possible to identify the one for whom the plate was engraved.

Arms: Arg. a greyhound courant gu. betw. 3 ravens ppr. within a bordure engr. gu. charged alternately with 4 roundels and 4 crosses pattés or.

Crest: A mailed arm embowed with naked hand holding an oak sprig.

Motto: Pas pour moi (Not for me).

Name: In script, below.

Style: Chippendale.
Unsigned.

WILLIAMS, JOHN C.

Coats with rampant lions are so frequently found that the derivation of the blazon is not easy to trace with certainty. There was, however, a coat with lion rampant, though with different details and crest, granted in 1767 to a John Williams, of Boston, Inspector-General of North America, and possibly John C. was of this family, though there was a John Chester Williams who was of Yale, 1765, and died, 1819, who might possibly be the owner. There are two states of this plate.

Arms: Az. a lion rampant arg.

Crest: A cock of the woods.

Motto: Cognosce Occasionem (Recognize the opportunity).

Name: In script, below.

Style: Ribbon and wreath.

Signed: N H Scp, in script.

The second state has an entirely different scroll and motto, the latter being 'Pauca Respexi Pauciora Despexi' (I have looked up at few things, I have looked down at fewer).
Unsigned or cut off.

WILSON, DAVID

One of this name was Commissary of the Army in 1769.

Arms: Gu. a wolf rampant between 3 estoiles of six points arg.

Crest: A wolf's head erased.

PLATE XXVII

Nathaniel Hurd's Bookplates

Name: Below, in script, which does not resemble Hurd's style.
Style: Chippendale decoration, the whole enclosed in a border
    garlanded with corner shells.
Allen No. 945.

With the exception of the name, the plate, though unsigned, strongly resembles Hurd, although the border is unusual with him.

This is a second state of the James Wilson plate, the first name having been erased and re-engraved and a flourish added to the 'W.'

WILSON, JAMES

Jurist, signer of the Declaration of Independence; born in Scotland, 1742; married Rachel Bird, 1771; died, 1798, having lived mostly in Pennsylvania.

This plate is the first state of the David Wilson plate. The cartouche and Chippendale decoration are almost identical with the John Vassall plate.

Unsigned, but probably by Hurd.
Allen No. 946.

Portraits of Nathaniel Hurd

NATHANIEL was fortunate in being painted twice by Copley, even though one of the portraits was unfinished.

The heads on both pictures are completed, however, and give a good idea of the man, who appears to have had a stocky figure with a nearly round face, dark eyes, well-marked eyebrows, a straight nose, a strong jaw, and rather a large mouth with full lips. In both portraits he is wearing a large and baggy velvet cap. His hair is cut very short; he is clean-shaven and has a powerful figure.

In the unfinished portrait, which is believed to be a study for the other, he is in working clothes with his right arm bare, a shirt open at the throat and what appears to be a leather waist-coat or jacket.

The finished picture depicts him with the same open shirt, but with a loose jacket or dressing-gown with full sleeves showing linen at the wrists. He is sitting close to a table with his hands folded, and resting near his right arm are two leather-bound volumes, the larger one of which, in sheepskin, is entitled in legible gilt letters, 'Display of Heraldry Guillim.'

Undoubtedly this is the book from which Nathaniel obtained his heraldic data in great part, and from the fact that it was included in the portrait, it would appear that perhaps he preferred being depicted as an engraver rather than as a silversmith. This portrait is a fine example of Copley's painting and is now in the Cleveland Museum of Art, obtained from the Furnass family of Massachusetts.

Nathaniel's sister Anne married John Furnass, now spelled Furness, and inherited the portraits, one of which was sold by her descendants not a great many years ago, the unfinished one being now on loan at the Pennsylvania Museum in Philadelphia, and owned by Horace H. Furness Jayne, Wallingford, Pennsylvania, who inherited it.

Furnass himself was a portrait painter of considerable ability in that period.

The unfinished likeness is described in Bulletin # 19 of the Pennsylvania Museum, and the finished portrait in the publication of the Cleveland Museum of Art of March, 1923. It is to be noted that the expression of the face in the latter is not as pleasing as in the sketch. In fact, it almost seems as if the finished likeness was of a little later date, when perhaps Hurd had changed slightly.

Mentioned in Nathaniel's will is a miniature of himself painted by his friend Copley, which has been the object of search for a long time, and only found recently by Professor J. M. Phillips in the Furness family. It is the property of Miss Emily Furness, of Brookline, who inherited it in direct line from her ancestress, Ann Hurd. This miniature is very small and is no doubt intended for Nathaniel, as one can tell by the distinctive cap which also appears on his head in both life-size oil portraits. It is unsigned, but doubtless by Copley.

Another miniature on copper and signed with Copley's initials 'ISC' is also in Miss Furness's possession, but whether it is of Nathaniel or of Captain John Furnass, as appears in pencil on the back, is uncertain. It is considerably larger than

[139   ]

the miniature just described; it is better executed, and, so far as the features go, it resembles Nathaniel more than the other one, so that he may well have been the subject.

If this is the case, we have two miniatures of Nathaniel, and the problem of why he mentioned only one in his will, written shortly before his death, presents itself. However, as neither of the much more important oil portraits was mentioned, this question is probably of no great moment.

A copy of the finished portrait done by John Furnass, is also in the possession of his descendant, Miss Furness.

Another portrait is a copy of the 'mezzotinto,' done by Richard Jennys, which was referred to in the *New England Magazine* of 1832 in an article on Nathaniel, from which we quote as follows:

> There is an original picture of him in the possession of one of his relatives at Medford, Mass. From that picture a man by the name of Jennys (of whom we can learn very little) engraved a likeness in Mezzotinto and of that mezzotinto, the lithographic print which accompanies this memoir is, as near as the different modes of engraving will admit, an exact copy.

The lithograph in the magazine of 1832 and another copy of that lithograph, found in *Ex Libris* of Washington in 1896, have long been known, but they do not resemble either of Copley's paintings, except perhaps in the hat.

The New York Public Library has a wash drawing of Nathaniel taken either from the mezzotint or the magazine, but none of these are of any artistic importance, and hardly worth reproduction here, especially as the life-size Copley portraits, which are reproduced, are of real value artistically.

Benjamin Hurd

SILVERSMITH

1739-1781

Benjamin Hurd, Silversmith

O F THE fourteen children born to Jacob the Goldsmith and his wife Elizabeth Mason the tenth child was Benjamin, who was born in Boston May 12, 1739, and baptized in the New South Church on August 12 of that year. His wife, whom he married in Roxbury on April 13, 1774, was Priscilla, daughter of Jonathan and Susanna (Gore) Crafts, who was born January 9, 1743, and who died at the age of sixty-eight in Boston November 23, 1811.

They had two children, Benjamin, Jr., whose dates are lacking, as well as any information about him, and Sarah, who was born November 16, 1779, and who married Ebenezer Rhodes, and died June 13, 1870.

Benjamin, the son of Jacob, became a silversmith, and no doubt was an apprentice in his father's shop, as he was nineteen years old when Jacob died, and there worked with his brother Nathaniel, who was ten years older.

John Hurd, who was older than Nathaniel by two years and was the potential head of the family after Jacob died, was appointed by the Court on the petition of Benjamin, then a minor, to be his guardian, to manage 'all and singular such Part and Portion of Estate as accrues to me in Right of my Hon^d Father Jacob Hurd late of Roxbury in Y^e County afores^d

[143]

Benjamin Hurd, Silversmith

Goldsmith.' This he signed and 'set my Hand and Seal this 9th Day of March Anno Domini, 1759, and in the Thirty-second Year of the Reign of Our Sovereign Lord King George Yᵉ Second over Great Britain, Etc.

(Signed)   Benjᵃ Hurd'

There is very little information available on the life and activities of Benjamin. He is spoken of as an heraldic artist and reference is made to him in the *Heraldic Journal* (Vol. 4, p. 192), which says that armorial paintings bearing the name of Benjamin Hurd, Jr., have been shown their committee. This might refer to the son of Benjamin about whom we know practically nothing, though it is improbable, as he is believed to have been a bookbinder.

Benjamin is also said to have been an engraver and a pupil of Copley, and the same reference above states that 'he made many works of art in both gold and copper, silver and bronze, many of fine and intricate design and workmanship representing historical places and events, besides coats of arms.'

In an article of the New England Historic and Genealogical Society *Journal* for April, 1886, by Lichtenstein, whose information on bookplates was most extensive, Benjamin was referred to as an engraver and designer of bookplates. Consequently, it is probable that one or more plates of his may be found when the Lichtenstein Collection is dispersed.

All this sounds quite specific, but after a diligent search the only works of Benjamin's which have so far been found are fifteen pieces of silver, comprising two baptismal basins, one cream jug, and twelve spoons, though no doubt others will be found. In fact it is believed there was a teapot in Ansonia, but it cannot be located now.

These show evidence of excellent workmanship and will be found described in detail in the silver index herein (page 53).

PLATE XXVIII

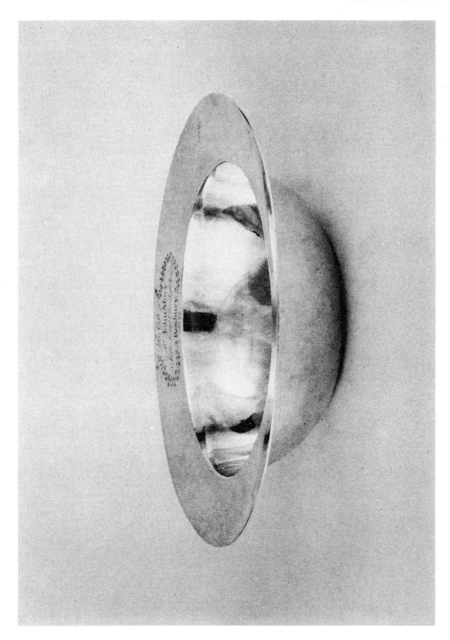

Benjamin Hurd, Silversmith

It seems strange, however, that if he were so talented more of his works should not be in existence today. There are a few facts about him which can be established, however.

Benjamin Hurd was one of a committee of nine chosen on November 26, 1774, to see that 'The acts and resolves of the Grand American Congress and of the Provincial Congress were duly executed so far as relates to this Town.'

He was Town Treasurer of Boston from 1772 to 1776, as stated in Winsor's *Memorial History*, page 330, which gives a reproduction of his autograph as follows:

He lived in Roxbury, but though we find no entry in the Book of Possessions or in the Registry of Deeds which relates to him, his inventory states that he owned 'a third part of a Dwelling House in Court Square near the State House,' of which his share was appraised at £150. This property must have been inherited by him and his two sisters, Elizabeth Henchman and Ann Furnass, under the residuary clause in Nathaniel's will, Benjamin's share being one-third.

Benjamin died, as recorded in the inscription on the stone in the Granary Burying Ground, which runs, 'In memory of Mr. Benjamin Hurd, Goldsmith, son of the late Capt. Jacob Hurd, who died at Roxbury, 2d day of June 1781, aged 42 years, and is here interred.' Close by him lies his brother-in-law, Daniel Henchman, who died six years earlier.

Benjamin probably died intestate and his brother John with two goldsmiths, Benjᵃ Burt and Zachariah Brigden, with one Clark, were appointed appraisers. (Suffolk Probate, Lib. LIV, p. 176 and LXXX, pp. 295, 315, and 592.)

Benjamin Hurd, Silversmith

The total of the estate amounted to £303–2–10, a not inconsiderable sum for those days, but the chief interest in the inventory is the complete list of the shop tools and furniture that a silversmith of those times possessed. These Benjamin inherited partly under his brother Nathaniel's will, and they included, no doubt, some of his father Jacob's tools.

The marks so far discovered on Benjamin's silver are as follows:

13. ⟦B.↑H⟧   Initials in Roman caps, arrowhead between in rectangle.

14. ⟦B·HURD⟧   Initial and surname, pellet between capitals in double rectangle.

15. ⟦B.Hurd.⟧   Initial and surname capitals, pellet between, 'urd' semiscript, in long oval.

In the Masonic Museum of Boston, there have recently been discovered three copies of a diploma engraved and signed by 'Brother B. Hurd del.' which is the first of his engravings so far found.

This Master Mason Diploma was designed to be issued to Thirty-Second Degree Masons by various lodges, and by filling in the blanks in the text by hand, it certified that the recipient possessed such a title. One of these was issued in 1796, and two in 1797.

The design of the Certificate, which was 15⅛″ wide and 13½″ high, consists of an arch supported by two Corinthian columns standing on a tessellated pavement with two composite columns in the background.

In the foreground are three steps, on which are grouped several Masonic emblems, and at each end of the steps are two pedestals, surmounted by figures of children holding other Masonic insignia.

The engraving is well done.

Partial List of References Consulted

Allen, Charles D.: *American Bookplates.*
American Antiquarian Society, Collections and Publications.
Avery, C. Louise: *Early American Silver.*
                The Clearwater Collection.
Baker, William S.: *American Engravers.*
Bigelow, Francis H.: *Historic Silver of the Colonies.*
Bolton, Charles K.: *Bolton's American Armory.*
Book of Possessions: In Boston Record Commissioner's 2d Report.
Boston: Cemetery Records.
        Massachusetts State Records.
        Newspapers of the period.
        Probate Records.
        Record Commissioners' Reports.
        Registry of Deeds.
        Various Church Records.
Bridgman, Thomas: *Pilgrims of Boston.*
Buck, John H.: *Old Plate.*
Burke, John: *Encyclopaedia of Heraldry.*
Catalogues: Various sales and exhibitions.
Clarke, Hermann F.: *John Coney.*
              Jeremiah Dummer.
Currier, E. M.: *Marks of Early American Silversmiths.*
Dictionary of American Biography.
Dow, George Francis: *The Arts and Crafts in New England.*
Drake, Samuel A.: *Old Landmarks of Boston.*
Drake, Samuel G.: *The History and Antiquities of Boston.*
Dunlap, William: *A History of the Arts of Design in the United States.*
Ellis, Arthur B.: *History of the First Church in Boston.*
Fielding, Mantle: *Dictionary of American Sculptors,* etc.
French, Hollis: *A List of Early American Silversmiths,* etc.
Genealogies: Various Family Genealogies
Guillim, John: *Display of Heraldry.*
Heraldry: *The Heraldic Journal.*
        Chute Pedigree.
        Gore Roll.

Partial List of References Consulted

Miner Pedigree.

Promptuarium Armorum.

Howe, Mark A. DeW.: *Boston, the Place and the People.*

Hurd, Dena D.: *History and Genealogy of the Hurd Family.*

Jones, E. Alfred: *The Old Silver of American Churches.*

Massachusetts Historical Society: Collections and Publications.

Morison, Samuel E.: *Tercentennial History of Harvard.*

                        Three Centuries of Harvard and other writings.

New England Historic and Genealogical Register.

Papworth, John W.: *Ordinary of British Armorials.*

Prince, Thomas: *Chronological History of New England.*

Roberts, Oliver A.: *History of the Military Company of the Massachusetts*
                 (now Ancient and Honorable Artillery Company).

Savage, James: *A Genealogical Dictionary of the First Settlers of New England.*

Sewall, Samuel: Letter Book, 1685 to 1734.

                Diary, 1674 to 1729.

Stauffer, David M.: *American Engravers.*

Thwing, Annie H.: *The Crooked and Narrow Streets of Boston.*

Winsor, Justin: *The Memorial History of Boston.*

THIS AND THE FOLLOWING PAGES ARE RESERVED FOR EN-
TERING DATA REGARDING SILVER, ENGRAVINGS, AND BOOK-
PLATES WHICH MAY BE DISCOVERED AFTER PUBLICATION

Since going to press, the Curator of the Garvan Collection
has found reason to question the authenticity of the mark
on their coffee pot by Jacob Hurd, No. 111 in the text.

ADDENDA

THE WALPOLE SOCIETY

Jacob Hurd
AND HIS SONS
Nathaniel & Benjamin

Silversmiths
1702 — 1781

By

HOLLIS FRENCH, S.B.
Member of the Walpole Society
Member of the American Antiquarian Society

PRINTED BY THE RIVERSIDE PRESS FOR THE WALPOLE SOCIETY
MCMXLI

SHORTLY after the publication of the book, pieces which had not been included in it came to the author's notice. To make the book as complete as possible, he arranged the additional material, intending to present it in a leaflet which could be laid inside the cover.

After Mr. French's death, the Society was fortunate in securing the help of Mrs. Yves H. Buhler of the Boston Museum of Fine Arts, who has edited what the author intended to add, and has brought it to the point where, rather than wait longer for possible further discoveries, it would seem to be of sufficient completeness to be of value to the original subscribers.

Addenda

[3]

Mrs. Rebecca Townsend, dated 1747. Included in it is a pair of casters weighing 7 ounces 11 pennyweight. This pair is undoubtedly the very pair in the collection of Philip Hammerslough, as the latter are engraved 'R T' in contemporary capitals and now weigh 7 ounces 4 pennyweight; the difference of 7 pennyweight showing the amount of silver eroded by wear in the intervening ninety-three years.

37   112. Privately owned.

    112 and 114. Catalogue reference should be to number rather than to page.

38   120a. *Cream jug.* Pear-shaped body, three slipper feet, serrated rim, double scroll handle. H, to top of handle 4"; H, to lip 3 1/4"; DB, 2 1/4". Mark # 4. Engraved on front of body 'S Holland' in crude letters with floriations, and a crest: a mailed arm embowed. Owner, Edmund Bury, Esq., Philadelphia.

38   124a. *Cup.* Beaker shape with flaring lip and base moulding, plain strap handle. H, 4"; DM, 3 3/4"; DB, 3 3/16". Mark # 2 near handle and on bottom. Engraved on bottom in early script, 'Phebe Collman' (she married Barzillai Folger who was born c. 1705), from whom it has descended to its present owner. Owner, Miss Laura Howland Dudley, Cambridge, Massachusetts.

39   131. *Dish.* The authenticity of this piece is questioned.

    132. *Jug.* This piece was made by Jesse Churchill, for a descendant of Nathaniel Curtis, one of whose descendants was to marry a descendant of Jacob Hurd.

40   143. *Cabot* should read *Caleb.*

    143a. *Mug.* Like above. H, 5 3/4"; DM, 4 1/4"; DB, 5". Marks # 1 on base, # 2 on rim. Engraved 'S/F H' on handle. This has a capacity of 1 3/8 quarts. Owner, Miss Mary G. Gilman, Brunswick, Maine.

    146. Engraved with the Oliver arms, but given by descendants in the Dawes family to the Museum.

    48. Should read # 148.

    149a. *Porringer.* D, 5 1/4"; H, 2"; L, handle 2 5/8"; Wt, 7 oz. 6 dwt. Marks # 3 on side near top, # 1 on back of handle. Engraved on handle 'P C' in early capitals for Prudence Chester (see # 319). Owner, Mrs. Fred Remington Greene, Seattle, Washington.

    151. *David* should read *Dorothy.*

41   167a. *Porringer.* D, 4 1/2"; H, 1 5/8"; L, handle 2 3/8". Mark # 4 on back of handle. Engraved on handle:
    M P (Mercy Prescott to her granddaughter
      to Rebecca Prescott, born May 20, 1742, who married Roger Sherman.
    R P Their daughter Mehitabel married Daniel Barnes, whose descendant, Mrs. John French, of New York, presented the piece to Yale University.)

[4   ]

And on sides: 'Mrs. Roger Sherman 1774/Mrs. Daniel Barnes 1844.' Owner, Yale University.

167b. *Porringer.* D, 5 1/8"; H, 1 7/8"; Wt, 7 oz. 5 1/2 dwt. Mark #1 on back of handle. Engraved 'P' for the Phillips family, from whom it has descended. Owner, Mrs. James M. Beale, Wellesley, Massachusetts.

42 172a. *Rapier.* Mark #3 or #4. Original owner, Colonel Thomas Noyes (1648–1730). Owner, F. L. N., Massachusetts (illustrated in magazine *Antiques* for January, 1940).

42 176–177. Numbers of casters should read #100–101.

177a and b. *Pair of circular salts,* on three legs, with trefoil body joinings. Moulded rim. D, 2 1/2"; H, 1 1/2". Mark #4. Engraved with script 'I G' on which was later superimposed an old English 'B.' Owner, Norman Bemis Chandler, Esq., Cambridge, Massachusetts.

181a. *Sauceboat.* Like above. L, 7 3/4"; W, 4 3/8"; H, bowl 2 1/4". Mark #4. Engraved with crest. Owner, William H. Putnam, Esq., Hartford, Connecticut.

44 216a. *Spoon.* Like above. L, 8". Mark #5. Crest on back of handle: on a torse a griffin's head pierced through the neck by an arrow, point to sinister. Owner, R. P. Pauly, Esq., Boston, Massachusetts.

220a. *Spoon.* Like above, with shell on bowl. L, 4 13/16". Mark #3. Engraved 'RW' on back of handle and (later) 1758. Owner, William David Anderson, Esq., Cambridge, Massachusetts.

220b. *Spoon.* Like above. L, 4". Mark #4. Engraved 'A T.' Owner, Mrs. J. Edward Brooks, Milton, Massachusetts.

45 231a. *Spoon.* Single drop and rib front. L, 4 9/16". Mark #3. Engraved 'E B' on back of handle. Owner, MFA, Boston, the gift of Arthur D. Foss in 1939.

231b. *Spoon.* Like above. L, 4 7/8". Mark #4. Engraved 'E P,' device above. Owner, William David Anderson, Esq., Cambridge, Massachusetts.

232a. *Spoon.* Mote. Like above with double drop on oval bowl, geometric piercings, and engraved tulip motive. L, 5 3/16". Mark #3 on stem. Owner, Garvan.

243a. *Tankard.* With acorn finial. H, 6" to lip, 7 3/4" to finial top; DM, 4"; DB, 4 3/4". Mark #4. Engraved on handle in old capitals 'I H O B' ('O' added later), and below 'D' for Dunning, in later engraving but old. The early initials probably stand for Jeremiah H. O'Brien, who originally bought the tankard. He was born in Kittery, Maine, in 1744 and died in Machias, Maine, in 1818, after serving with brilliance in the United States Navy. His daughter, Mary, married a Mr. Dunning, and hence the added initial on the handle. (See his *Life* in the Boston Public Library.) Engraved with impaled coat-of-arms: Baron: per Chevron in Chief two birds rising; Femme: a cross potent, on a canton the badge of a baronet; Crest: a dove rising. (Tinctures are not indicated.) Owner, Anonymous.

[5]

Addenda

47 265a and b. *Pair of tankards.* With bell-shaped finials; spouts added. (*a*) H, 8″; DB, 5 1/4″. Mark # 2 at left of handle. Engraved in decorated double circle in italics, 'The Gift/of Mr. Ebenezer Metcalf/to the First Church/ in Lebanon.' (*b*) H, 7 3/4″; DB, 5 1/8″. Marks # 6 at left of handle and # 4 on lid. Engraved in undecorated double circle, 'The Gift of / Mrs. Sarah Phelps/to the first Church/in Lebanon/1746.' Owner, First Church in Lebanon.

49 289. This piece is octagonal on four scroll feet. Addenda: A careful examination of the surface of the erased arms and crest by Professor Phillips, of Yale University, results in his belief that the arms and crest were those of the Colman family and were similar to the arms on the famous monteith by John Coney in the Garvan Collection. The ancestors of the previous owners of the monteith and the present owners of the tray were related.

50 296a. *Tray.* Small salver on four feet. W, about 6 1/2″. Mark # 4. Engraved in early capitals 'C/I S' (for the Chauncy family). Owner, Mrs. Seth Low Pierrepont, Ridgefield, Connecticut.

51 301a. *Can.* Like above. H, 5″; D, 3 1/2″. Mark # 9. Engraved on handle 'L/L S.' Inscribed, 'Elizabeth Meigs to Amelia Meigs Whaples.' Owner, Heywood H. Whaples, Esq., Hartford, Connecticut.

301b. *Can.* H, 4 3/4″ Mark # 10. Engraved with coat-of-arms, quartered: 1. Three hearts. 2. A crosslet, 3. Three nails. 4. A bugle-horn (?). The arms show no indications of tinctures, according to which the three hearts might refer to Cramond, Massey, or Kirkhoven. Mr. Bolton also records a Hart coat-of-arms of this design. Owner, Mrs. Henry Ellett, Richmond, Virginia.

304. Engraved with Howard arms to match teapot # 321.

52 318a. *Sugar scissors,* terminating in shell pattern on which appears an engraved eagle. L, 4 1/2″. Mark # 10. Owner, Detroit Institute of Arts, the gift of Robert H. Tannahill in 1940.

318b. *Tankard.* Pear-shape on moulded base, with moulded applied midband. Scroll handle with rounded body drop and disc tip. Domed and moulded cover, open scroll thumb piece. H, 7 7/8″; DB, 4 5/16″. Mark # 9 at left of handle. Engraved with two coats-of-arms impaled: Baron: Quartered: 1 and 4, Vert a chevron argent between three griffin's heads erased.... 2 and 3, Or a chevron vert between three eagles displayed.... Femme: Or a chevron gules between three eagles displayed.... Crest, none; replaced by a basket of fruit. Owner, Mrs. Henry C. Clark, Prides Crossing, Massachusetts.

319. The original owner was Prudence Chester (1699–1780), wife of Colonel John Stoddard, of Northampton, Massachusetts.

321. Date should read 1766.

53 337. *Spoon.* Feather edge with short ribbon back at end of handle, drop and shell on back of bowl. L, 4 11/16″. Mark # 13. In fine condition except that initials on the front of the handle have been filed off damaging the feather

[6]

edge on both sides at that place. Owner, George B. Cutten, Esq., Hamilton, New York.

To be added before the paragraph headed 'Dies':

The Brown Seal. In the publications of the Rhode Island Historical Society Collections, XXII: 1, January, 1929, there is a note on page 62 of arms of the Brown family, of Providence, which are entirely different from those on the Bookplate mentioned on page 96 herein.

We quote from the late Howard M. Chapin, of Providence, who wrote the text of the 1929 publication:

'The earliest record in regard to the use of arms by the Chad Brown family of Providence is a letter written by Moses Brown, of Providence, September 2, 1763, to Benjamin Burt, of Boston, in which letter Brown ordered a mustard pot to be engraved with "The Arms, a chevron between three Lyons paws erected within a bordure and an Eagle displayed and the same that Mr. N. Hurd Ingraved on a seal for me sometime since."' (Moses Brown Papers, Vol. 1, in the Rhode Island Historical Society Library.) No example of this seal by Nathaniel Hurd has yet been found.

The Seal of Dartmouth College. From Chase, *History of Dartmouth College:* 'The meeting of the board was held August 25th (1773). Besides other things, the College seal was adopted, agreeably to its impression upon a steel die, engraved by Mr. Nathaniel Hurd, of Boston, and presented, with a suitable screw-press, at this time by Hon. George Jaffrey.* It bears within, upon a shield projecting, a pine grove on the right, whence proceed natives toward an edifice of two stories on the left, which bears in a label over the roof the words *Vox clamantis in deserto;* the whole supported by Religion on the right, and Justice on the left, and bearing a triangle irradiate with the Hebrew words . . . El Shaddai, . . . God Almighty. The motto is the same that was proposed for this purpose by Wheelock to the English trust in March, 1770, when, ignorant as yet of their unfavorable attitude toward the College, he requested them to devise a seal.'

This is the only reference to be found of the maker of the seal which measures 2 5/16" by 2 5/8", and the College records do not mention Hurd's name. However, Hurd signed his initials to the engraving he executed on the monteith made by his brother-in-law, Daniel Henchman, and inscribed: 'His Excellency John Wentworth, Esq./Governor of the Province of New Hampshire/And those Friends who accompanied him/To Dartmouth College the first Commencement 1771/In Testimony of their Gratitude and good

---

* 'Mr. Hurd was the most eminent and skilful engraver of his day. He was a brother of Colonel John Hurd, of Haverhill, and inherited his skill from his father (see Grafton County Bar Proceedings, 1888). The original die is still in use, and in perfect condition. The press given by Mr. Jaffrey, though still preserved, ceased to be used in 1876, when the seal was fitted with a male die by the successor of Mr. Hurd, and mounted upon a modern lever press. Since then diplomas have received the impression on the parchment itself, and the ancient blue ribbon has been discarded. For about two years (1817–19), the seal being detained by the university party, a temporary die, with a different device, was used.'

Addenda

Wishes/Present this to the Revd Eleazer Wheelock, D. D. President/And to his Successors in that Office.'

The Brown University Seal. Walter C. Bronson, in his *History of Brown University 1764–1914*, reports: 'The second meeting of the Corporation was held in Newport on the first Wednesday in September, 1765; twenty-five members were present, and much important business was done. The following entries on the records have peculiar interest: "A Seal for the College was ordered to be procured immediately by the Reverend Samuel Stillman with this Device: Busts of the King and Queen in Profile, Face to Face. Underneath George III. Charlotte. Round the Border, The Seal of the College in the Colony of Rhode Island and Providence Plantations in America."'

In the John Carter Brown Library is a receipted bill:

The Revd Mr Stillman to Nat Hurd D^r

To 1 Large Steel Seal .. £105 —

Rec^d ten Guineas in full

Nat. Hurd

To 100 wafers   3/Sterling

in wax

Nat. Hurd

The seal is 2 1/8″ in diameter. Mr. Lawrence C. Wroth states that the University does not possess the seal itself now, but has two impressions from it.

83   Change the first line in the fourth paragraph to read: 'Other American sources were consulted through late copies, as some of the originals cannot be viewed.'

86   In the first line substitute 'Russell' for 'Randall,' as John Hurd's second wife was named Mary Russell Foster.

88   In drawing of arms the trident should be shown in outline only, and stippled like the chief.

101   George and Lewis DeBlois were cousins, not brothers. Both were Loyalists. George DeBlois (1739/40–1799) Lewis DeBlois (1727–1799).

102   A pair of cans engraved with Dering arms was in existence a short time ago, but have not been traced. There is a question whether they were made by Jacob or Nathaniel, but, considering the latter's activities for the Dering family, it seems reasonable to assume they may be of his workmanship.

117   *Jarvis.* In June, 1940, the American Antiquarian Society obtained an original Leonard Jarvis bookplate signed by N. Hurd, a fine example from an early book.

139   John Mason Furnass, son of John and Ann (Hurd) Furnass, was the portrait painter and made the copy of the Copley mentioned on the following page. The miniature mentioned in the will was bequeathed to Elizabeth (Hurd) Henchman, whose daughter married Ann (Hurd) Furnass's son. The ivory miniature is traditionally by Copley, though technically unlike his signed ones.

[8   ]